ISLAM AND THE END TIMES

DR. GENE GURGANUS

Copyright @2010

All rights reserved. No portion of this book may be reproduced, stored in a retrieval system, or transmitted by any form or by any means—electronic, mechanical, photocopy, recording, scanning, or other—except for brief quotations in critical reviews or articles, without the prior permission of the publisher.

Published in Greenville, South Carolina by Truth Publishers
Printed by Lightning Source

All scripture references from the Holy Bible, King James Version.

Gurganus, Gene, 1929
Islam and the End Times / Gene Gurganus
p.cm
Eschatology, current events

ISBN 9781935507208

Cover art by Zach Fransen

Design by Caleb Greene

DEDICATION

This book is dedicated to **Elizabeth Jeanette English Gurganus.**

My wife of 56 years passed away on March 27, 2009, after suffering debilitating dementia for several years. Praise God, she lived well and she died well. Her last words, "I see the river and I see Jesus," gladdened our grieving hearts. In dedicating this book to her, I could fill volumes singing her praises. I will not do that. I will say she was a Proverbs 31 lady. Her husband, her three daughters, her three sons-in-law, her twenty grandchildren, and her fifteen (soon to be sixteen) great-grandchildren rise up and call her BLESSED. To this wonderful lady, who gave me her love and devotion, a beautiful family, and a warehouse full of good memories, I dedicate this book, *Islam and the End Times*.

TABLE OF CONTENTS

Dedication iii
Preface.. vi
Acknowledgements... viii
Foreword x
Introduction... xi

PART ONE

A STUDY OF THE END TIMES IN LIGHT OF THE BIBLE AND MUSLIM TRADITIONS

Chapter 1: Eschatology – The Study of End Times..................... 2
Chapter 2: The Coming of the Mahdi 12
Chapter 3: Identifying the Antichrist... 26
Chapter 4: The Mahdi and the Antichrist.................................... 40
Chapter 5: The Mahdi and the Antichrist –Continued................ 51
Chapter 6: The Mahdi and the Antichrist –Continued................ 62
Chapter 7: The Mahdi and the Antichrist –Continued................ 74
Chapter 8: Jesus in the Koran, the Hadith, and the Bible 86
Chapter 9: Dajjal – Monster or Savior? 98
Chapter 10: Antichrist's Empire – East or West?...................... 106
Chapter 11: Rome or Islam 116
Chapter 12: Day of the Lord 127
Chapter 13: The Harlot, Mystery Babylon and the Beast.......... 139
Chapter 14: Revived Islamic Empire – The Caliphate.............. 154

PART TWO

A BIBLICAL RESPONSE TO PROPHETICAL TRUTH

Chapter 15: A Realistic View of the World 168
Chapter 16: Will America be Islamized?.. 178
Chapter 17: Will America Be Islamized? – Continued 187

End Notes 198
Glossary 207
Bibliography 209
Personal Index 215
Subject Index 220

PREFACE

Many people have asked me "How does Islam figure in the end time scenario?" I must admit, for the most part, I have given an obscure answer to the effect that Islam will certainly play a substantial role. However, there was a gnawing suspicion that Islam would be a dominant force, but I had not been able to put it all together. In the course of my ministry of 59 years, I believe the Lord has directed my attention to crucial books at critical times that have helped me to a better understanding of Biblical truth.

Two books have recently come to my attention dealing with Islam, prophecy, the Antichrist and related subjects. First, *God's War on Terror, Islam, Prophecy and the Bible*, by Walid Shoebat, a converted Palestinian Muslim terrorist, and *The Islamic Antichrist – the Shocking Truth about the Real Nature of the Beast*, by Joel Richardson. Both books are well written and are carefully documented from original sources. Each author is hermeneutically sound, i.e., very careful in the interpretation of Scripture. These are God-honoring and Bible-believing men. These two books have helped me crystallize what I believe the Bible teaches about how Islam will play a dominant role in the end times.

The title of this book, *Islam and the End Times*, explains what the book is about. Eschatology, the study of last things will be examined both from the Christian and the Islamic viewpoint. Muslims are looking for the Mahdi, their Messiah, and Christians are looking for the return of Christ. First, we relate what Muslim tradition says about the Mahdi. Next, we give the Biblical teaching concerning the Antichrist. The similarities between the Mahdi and the Antichrist boggle the mind. We will carefully compare Muslim tradition and Biblical teaching concerning these two interesting personalities.

Daniel's revelation concerning Nebuchadnezzar's image will be examined in detail, including the countries playing vital roles. A historical survey of Islam's history, its decline and its rise, will be given. We will close with an update on Islamic jihad in America and what demographics teach us about the future of Europe and the West.

Needless to say, this book will be controversial. It will be breaking new ground and introducing new possibilities. I have no bones to pick with other prophecy teachers. If they choose to disagree with my conclusions, we will still be friends and brothers in Christ. My motive is earnestly to seek, to the best of my ability, to determine what the Bible teaches as to how God will orchestrate the events leading to the culmination of human history.

Daily, Americans face Islam, jihad, shariah law, moderate Muslims, radical Muslims and much more. Ignorance on the one hand and the news blackout by liberal media on the other leaves most Americans vulnerable. All these matters will get our attention. My desire is to share complex issues simply, in a way everyone can understand and appreciate. Whether I am right or wrong, I assure you that this will be an interesting read.

Gene Gurganus
Taylors, South Carolina

ACKNOWLEDGMENTS

When it comes to writing and publishing books, I certainly stand on the shoulders of others. I would like to acknowledge those who have helped me, both with the subject matter and the editing.

First, I would like to thank those who have researched Islamic traditions, the Koran, and the sayings of Muslim scholars. Several books have been extremely helpful and I thank these authors for their hard work. Walid Shoebat, *God's War on Terror –Islam, Prophecy, and the Bible;* Joel Richardson, *Islamic Antichrist—The Shocking Truth About the Real Nature of the Beast*; Mark Gabriel, *Islam and Terrorism—What the Quran really teaches about Christianity, violence and the goals of Islamic jihad*; Jim Murk, *Islam Rising— the Never Ending Jihad Against Christianity,* Volume one, *The Never Ending Jihad Against the Jews and Israel,* Volume two, *The Never Ending Jihad Against America and the West,* Volume three. All of these books have been exceedingly helpful, and I tried to give due credit to the authors.

Second, I am thankful for those who helped with the editing: Martha Knox, Jerry Gass, Bob Nestor, Lydia Gurganus Greene, George Law, and Jay Walsh, my fellow missionary from Bangladesh. Others have encouraged me in my endeavors: Pastor Jim Bailey, Rev. Bill Kinkade, Dr. Dick Knox, Dr. Jim Starr, and Dr. Jesse Eaton. Others too numerous to mention have read the manuscript as it was being written and have assured me that I was on the right track.

Third, I am grateful for Dr. Clayton Shumpert, pastor emeritus of Grace Baptist Church, West Columbia, SC, founder and former director of C.L.A.I.M. (Christian Laymen Assisting International Missions) for B.I.M.I (Baptist International Missions

Incorporated), and now serving as their international representative, for writing the Foreword. It is reassuring when men of Dr. Shumpert's experience and stature put a stamp of approval on your work.

Fourth, I want to thank those who defy the political correctness madness and dare to tell the truth about Islam. Nonie Darwish, a Muslim shahid's (martyr) daughter's enlightening book, *Now They Call Me Infidel – Why I Renounced Jihad for America, Israel, and the War on Terror*; David Gaubatz's *Muslim Mafia – Inside the Secret Underworld that's Conspiring to Islamize America;* Robert Spencer's *The Complete Infidel's Guide to the Koran;* Dr. Anis Shorosh's *Islam Revealed – A Christian Arab's View of Islam;* Dr. Daniel Pipes', *Militant Islam Reaches America*; Steven Emerson's *American Jihad – The Terrorists Living Among Us*; David Horowitz's Freedom Center; and Brigitte Gabriel's Act for America are all true American patriots. Praise God that many more individuals and organizations see the danger and are alerting the American people as to what is going on. Pray that the Lord will protect them from those who would do them harm.

Fifth, I am indebted to Lightning Source, Inc. for printing this book. My grandsons, Aaron and Caleb Greene helped me ready the manuscript for publishing. Zac Fransen did a beautiful work on the cover. I will always be grateful for their assistance.

Sixth, and most importantly, I thank my God (Father, Son and Holy Spirit) for hearing my earnest prayers and graciously enabling me to finish the task of writing this book. Pray with me that God would use it to enlighten God's people to prayerful action.

Gene Gurganus
Taylors, SC
2010

FOREWORD

Every sincere Christian will want to read this book. It is not just another book about Bible prophecy. It is a startling book about the place of Islam in the end time. The author is very qualified to write this treatise for many reasons. First, he is an experienced author who has written eight books. Also, he is a real student who doggedly, systematically goes about to prove his premise. He is also qualified academically. He has three degrees, B.A. in Bible, M. Div., and a Doctor of Ministry. He is qualified by experience. He served 17 years as a missionary in Chittagong, Bangladesh. He studied Islamic beliefs, read the Koran extensively, and had a successful ministry among the Muslim people.

The reader should know that this book is written by one who loves the Bible and believes in its veracity without reservation. Even if you don't understand or agree with his position about the Antichrist, you must know that it comes from the heart of a serious student of God's Word. Read it slowly and prayerfully. Read with an open mind. Very few authors have pointed out the role of Islam when the Antichrist is revealed. The evidence is clear. It will be difficult to refute the facts of the book. The author is a man of impeccable character. He deserves a hearing. He is willing to stand alone if necessary to present truth. He is worthy of our commendation and applause.

B. Clayton Shumpert, D.D.

INTRODUCTION

I relate this background information so you will know where I am coming from.

Let's go back 59 years. Incredible changes have rocked our world during this period. I go back 59 years because in 1950 I was born into the family of God. In 1951 was called into the Gospel ministry. Since that time I have been an avid student of God's Word and other relevant books, as well as a keen observer of world events. A call to preach is a call to prepare. I loaded my gospel guns at Bob Jones University. Prior to my salvation and call, I had studied at Wake Forest University and at Penn State College of Optometry in Philadelphia.

At Bob Jones University I became active in Mission Prayer Band and, as a result of my praying God to send forth laborers to India, He sent me. After earning Bachelor of Arts and Master of Divinity degrees, I spent two years in pastoral and evangelistic work. On March 1, 1958, my wife, our four-year-old daughter, Lydia, and I sailed out of New York harbor on the SS Helenic Glory to begin a grand adventure, serving Christ in East Pakistan under the auspices of the Association of Baptists for World Evangelism. (Formerly East Bengal, India, East Pakistan became the independent nation of Bangladesh in 1971.)

For seventeen years I labored indefatigably to establish a beachhead in a pioneer mission field among Muslims. Thanks be to God and to the labors of my missionary and national co-workers, we left behind a functioning local church, a Bible correspondence school, and a camping program. Loss of hearing forced me to leave my ministry in East Pakistan.

For the next twenty years I served as the Southeastern representative of the Association of Baptists for World Evangelism (ABWE). I traveled worldwide promoting world evangelism and faith promise giving. All this time I was carefully observing the multitude of changes within our world and within the Church. One of the greatest, most far-reaching changes of the last 59 years has been the ascendancy of Islam.

During my missionary work among Muslims, I had no fear for my personal safety, even though I was threatened several times to stop my distributing literature. Once a Muslim shopkeeper tried unsuccessfully to take the tracts I was distributing out of my hands. And on one occasion, after one of our missionaries preached a message on five reasons we believe Christ is the Son of God, a large crowd of Muslims bricked our headquarters.

One day, a Muslim cleric, with a full black beard and black piercing eyes, robed in white with a shawl draped around his head, approached me. He spoke this message to me in the Bengali language: "Listen to me. One day we Muslims will Islamize America!" At the time the thought of Muslims dominating these United States seemed ludicrous. But today there is a real possibility of that cleric's prophecy being fulfilled. Muslims leaders are publicly saying that by 2050 America will be a Muslim nation and by 2020 the inner cities of our great metropolises will be predominantly Muslim.

And what about Europe? Libya's Khadafi says Europe will fall to Islam without a battle. How is this possible? Demographics! In France, the average birthrate for French couples is 1.5; for Muslim families, 8! At present, 30 percent of babies being born in Europe are Muslim. Twenty years down the road, Europe as we know it will cease to exist. Eurabia will have replaced it.

I bring these facts to your attention as they definitely relate to the end times and how we interpret what the Bible and the Koran teach concerning countries and peoples involved in the climactic events that lie ahead. I do not ask you to agree with my conclusions. I only ask you to read with a mind open to new data.

I opened this rather lengthy introduction mentioning momentous changes occurring before our eyes. Who would have thought a man born of a Kenyan Muslim and an atheist mother from Kansas would be elected president of the United States of America? The revitalization of Islam after 500 years of stagnation causes us to reexamine our previous interpretations relating to the end times. I will do my best not to go off the deep end but to examine carefully the evidence. A good maxim is, "Always follow the truth."

PART ONE

A STUDY OF END TIMES IN LIGHT OF THE BIBLE AND MUSLIM TRADITIONS

For whatsoever things were written aforetime were written for our learning, that we through patience and comfort of the scriptures might have hope.

Romans 15:4

CHAPTER ONE
ESCHATOLOGY – THE STUDY OF END TIMES

We get our word eschatology from the Greek word *eschatos* which means furthest or last. In other words, it means the study of last things such as death, resurrection, immortality and judgment. Early in my ministry among Muslims I became aware that those who were serious about their religion and their holy books, the Koran and the Hadith, had an eschatological system very similar to ours as Christians. I learned that they were looking for a Messiah whom they called the Mahdi. Prior to his coming, the world would be filled with chaos. It was also interesting to learn that they were also expecting an unsavory character they called Dajjal. He could be equated with the Antichrist of the Bible. The Jesus of the Bible is called Isa.

The Koran teaches that Jesus did not die on the cross. Allah substituted someone else to die on the cross, and Isa was caught up to heaven.

> *And for their unbelief and for their having uttered against Marium a grievous calumny. And their saying: Surely we have killed the Messiah, Isa son of Marium, the apostle of Allah; and they did not kill him nor did they crucify him, but it appeared to them so (like Isa) and most surely those who differ therein are only in a doubt about it; they have no knowledge respecting it, but only follow a conjecture, and they killed him not for sure. Nay! Allah took him up to Himself; and Allah is Mighty, Wise.* (Surah 4.156-158)

In the Islamic scheme of things, Isa will return to earth, not as a Christian but as a Muslim, and will assist the Mahdi in defeating the Jews and Christians. Isa will personally kill the Dajjal, who is really our Christ. Islam will triumph and the religion of Mohammed will cover the earth as the waters cover the sea.

HOLY BOOKS OF ISLAM

As Christians we have only one authoritative book, the Bible, comprising sixty-six books, thirty-nine in the Old Testament and twenty-seven in the New Testament. Islam has two holy books, the Koran and the Hadith.

Muslims worldwide hold the Koran in the highest esteem. The word *Koran* means recitation. The angel Gabriel (Jibriel) allegedly dictated the words of Allah to Mohammed. Since Mohammed was illiterate, he memorized the messages and told them to others, who wrote them down on leaves, bones, skins, stones, pieces of paper, etc. These communications continued over a span of twenty years. After Mohammed's death, his companions collected the messages into the book now called the Koran.

Just as the Koran is the words of Allah to Mohammed, the Hadith, the Muslims' second most holy book, is the words of Mohammed spoken to his companions. Muslims do not look upon the Hadith as equal to the Koran, but according to B. D. Kateregga, famed Muslim scholar, "To the Muslims the importance of the Hadith ranks only second to the Koran."[1]

Hadith (Arabic) literally means "narrative." These are narrations originating from the words and deeds of Mohammed. Hadith are regarded by traditional schools of jurisprudence as important tools for understanding the Koran and in matters of jurisprudence. They were then evaluated and gathered into large collections mostly during the 8th and 9th centuries. These works are referred to in matters of Islamic law and history to this day.[2]

The Koran places great emphasis upon the last days. Muslims have five tenets of belief: belief in Allah, belief in the last day, belief in angels, belief in the Scripture, and belief in the prophets. In Islamic eschatology there are minor signs and major signs. The minor signs are nebulous but the major signs are the coming of the Ad-Dajjal, the Muslim Antichrist; the return of the Muslim Jesus, Isa Al Maseeh, and most importantly, the coming of the Muslim Savior, Al-Mahdi. Every true Muslim believes in these major signs and has full confidence of the ultimate victory of Islam. Each of the major signs listed above comes from quotes from the Hadith. So it can be said that Islamic eschatology comes from the Hadith, not the Koran.

Sad to say, Christendom for the most part, considers belief in the last days, i.e., the rapture of the church, the Tribulation period, the second coming of Christ in power and glory, and the establishment of Christ's kingdom on earth (Millennium) as optional, questionable or just unimportant.

I will hasten to say that those of us who believe in an inspired Bible find great hope and assurance that God is working all things according to His own purposes. Not one jot or tittle will fail until all things are accomplished according to His Word and His will. Listen to what our Lord Jesus Christ, who is the truth said, *"For verily I say unto you, Till heaven and earth pass, one jot or one tittle shall in no wise pass from the law, till all be fulfilled"* (Matthew 5:18).

OVERVIEW OF BIBLICAL ESCHATOLOGY

Before we explore in more depth Islamic eschatology, it would be helpful to give a quick overview of Biblical eschatology. The very first prophecy concerning a coming Deliverer from the effects of the Fall is Genesis 3:15. *"And I will put enmity between thee and the woman, and between thy seed and her seed; it shall bruise thy head, and thou shalt bruise his heel."* The Deliverer would be a human being, uniquely the seed of the woman by the virgin birth, (not the seed of man) who would be wounded by the Serpent (Satan) but who would crush the Serpent's head. This is exactly what happened at the cross.

The next important prophecy connects the seed of the woman to the family of Abraham.

Now the LORD had said unto Abram, Get thee out of thy country, and from thy kindred, and from thy father's house, unto a land that I will shew thee: And I will make of thee a great nation, and I will bless thee, and make thy name great; and thou shalt be a blessing: And I will bless them that bless thee, and curse him that curseth thee: and in thee shall all families of the earth be blessed. (Genesis 12:1-3)

Through Jacob, the grandson of Abraham, God began to build a nation from whom the Deliverer would come. Genesis 49:10, "*The sceptre shall not depart from Judah, nor a lawgiver from between his feet, until Shiloh come; and unto him shall the gathering of the people be.*" The point here is that the tribe of Judah, one of Jacob's twelve sons, will be the royal tribe, and from this tribe the king of Israel will come.

In David, God found a man after His own heart. David was from the tribe of Judah and in Psalm 89:3-4, "*I have made a covenant with my chosen, I have sworn unto David my servant, Thy seed will I establish for ever, and build up thy throne to all generations. Selah.*" God promises that David's kingdom shall be an everlasting kingdom.

Isaiah 9:6 expands the picture by teaching that the Deliverer will be a child born and will also be the Son of God who is the mighty God.

For unto us a child is born, unto us a son is given: and the government shall be upon his shoulder: and his name shall be called Wonderful, Counsellor, The mighty God, The everlasting Father, The Prince of Peace. Of the increase of his government and peace there shall be no end, upon the throne of David, and upon his kingdom, to order it, and to establish it with judgment and with justice from henceforth even for ever. The zeal of the LORD of hosts will perform this.

Then we find some amazing prophecies that have all been literally fulfilled. Micah 5:2 informs us where the ruler of Israel will be born.

But thou, Bethlehem Ephratah, though thou be little among the thousands of Judah, yet out of thee shall he come forth unto me that is to be ruler in Israel; whose goings forth have been from of old, from everlasting.

Isaiah 53:5 tells of the vicarious sufferings of the Messiah Deliverer. "*But he was wounded for our transgressions; he was bruised for our iniquities: the chastisement of our peace was upon him; and with his stripes we are healed.*" A thousand years before the practice of crucifixion was known, the Psalmist vividly describes the Deliverer's hands and feet being nailed to a cross. Psalm 22:16, "*For dogs have compassed me: the assembly of the wicked has inclosed me: they pierced my hands and my feet.*" Psalm 16:9-11 prophesies the final victory of the Deliverer over sin and death.

Therefore my heart is glad, and my glory rejoiceth: my flesh also shall rest in hope. For thou wilt not leave my soul in hell; neither wilt thou suffer thine Holy One to see corruption. Thou wilt shew me the path of life: in thy presence is fulness of joy; at thy right hand there are pleasures for evermore.

The beginning of the New Testament brings this all together with these opening words:

The book of the generation of Jesus Christ, the son of David, the son of Abraham. Abraham begat Isaac; and Isaac begat Jacob; and Jacob begat Judas and his brethren...And Jacob begat Joseph the husband of Mary, of whom was born Jesus, who is called Christ. (Matthew 1:1,2,16)

We dare not overlook the importance of the Jewish nation in God's scheme of redemption. God promised Abraham and his descendants the land of Canaan in Genesis 13:14-18.

And the LORD said unto Abram, after that Lot was separated from him, Lift up now thine eyes, and look from the place where thou art northward, and southward, and eastward, and westward: For all the land which thou seest, to thee will I give it, and to thy seed for ever. And I will make thy seed as the dust of the earth: so that if a man can number the dust of the earth, then shall thy seed also be numbered. Arise, walk through the land in the length of it and in the breadth of it; for I will give it unto thee. Then Abram removed his tent, and came and dwelt in the plain of Mamre, which is in Hebron, and built there an altar unto the LORD.

Although Muslims deny it, the Bible is very clear that the covenant made with Abraham continued through his son, Isaac, not the son of the handmaiden Hagar, Ishmael. Genesis 26:2-4 says,

And the LORD appeared unto him (Isaac), and said, Go not down into Egypt; dwell in the land which I shall tell thee of: Sojourn in this land, and I will be with thee, and will bless thee; for unto thee, and unto thy seed, I will give all these countries, and I will perform the oath which I sware unto Abraham thy father; And I will make thy seed to multiply as the stars of heaven, and will give unto thy seed all these countries; and in thy seed shall all the nations of the earth be blessed.

The sad history of Israel can be summed up in disobedience, dispersion and cursing. Moses says in Deuteronomy 28:64-66,

And the LORD shall scatter thee among all people, from the one end of the earth even unto the other; and there thou shalt serve other gods, which neither thou nor thy fathers have known, even wood and stone. And among these nations shalt thou find no ease, neither shall the sole of thy foot have rest: but the LORD shall give thee there a trembling heart, and failing of eyes, and sorrow of mind: And thy life shall hang in doubt before thee; and thou shalt fear day and night, and shalt have none assurance of thy life.

What an accurate description of the Jewish people through the centuries!

Fast forward to Jesus talking to His disciples as they looked at the golden splendor of Herod's temple in Jerusalem. Matthew 24:1, 2

And Jesus went out, and departed from the temple: and his disciples came to him for to shew him the buildings of the temple. And Jesus said unto them, See ye not all these things? verily I say unto you, there shall not be left here one stone upon another, that shall not be thrown down.

This statement raised many questions in the disciples' minds.

They asked, *"What will be the sign of thy coming, and of the end of the world?"* Jesus' reply included the coming of deceivers, false prophets, wars, earthquakes, pestilences, fierce persecution and slaughter of God's servants, and the preaching of the gospel worldwide. Then He spoke of the abomination of desolation spoken by

Daniel the prophet. This speaks of Antichrist invading the temple and proclaiming himself to be God. We will speak more of this later.

Then Jesus speaks of the great tribulation and the coming of the Son of man in power and glory. 2 Thessalonians 1:7-9 vividly describes how God is going to deal with His enemies.

And to you who are troubled rest with us, when the Lord Jesus shall be revealed from heaven with his mighty angels, In flaming fire taking vengeance on them that know not God, and that obey not the gospel of our Lord Jesus Christ: Who shall be punished with everlasting destruction from the presence of the Lord, and from the glory of his power.

Israel – and those who escaped the great tribulation – will turn to Christ as described in Zechariah 12:10,

And I will pour upon the house of David, and upon the inhabitants of Jerusalem, the spirit of grace and of supplications: and they shall look upon me whom they have pierced, and they shall mourn for him, as one mourneth for his only son, and shall be in bitterness for him, as one that is in bitterness for his firstborn.

In Matthew 24:31, Jesus' words indicate a triumphant regathering of his persecuted people from the ends of the earth. *"And he shall send his angels with a great sound of a trumpet, and they shall gather together his elect from the four winds, from one end of heaven to the other."*

BRIEF OVERVIEW OF THINGS TO COME

Briefly, let me give an overview of the end times according to the Bible. We are now in the church age, the age of grace. This period will end with the Rapture of the church, followed by the Judgment Seat of Christ. After the Rapture of the church, the Tribulation Period begins. During this time, Antichrist will make a seven-year covenant with Israel and will gain worldwide support of his policies. He breaks the covenant after three-and-one-half years and starts a holocaust against Jews and Tribulation saints.

At the end of the Tribulation Period, Christ returns in glory and power, casting the Antichrist and the False Prophet into the bottomless pit. Matthew 25:31-46 speaks of the Judgment of the Nations, in which the nations will be judged according to how they treated the persecuted Jews during the Tribulation Period. The sheep nations, those who were good to Israel, will gain access into the millennial earth; the goat nations, those who persecuted Israel, will go into everlasting punishment.

Revelation 20:4-5 speaks of the Tribulation martyrs who were beheaded by the Antichrist.

> *And I saw thrones, and they sat upon them, and judgment was given unto them: and I saw the souls of them that were beheaded for the witness of Jesus, and for the word of God, and which had not worshipped the beast, neither his image, neither had received his mark upon their foreheads, or in their hands; and they lived and reigned with Christ a thousand years. But the rest of the dead lived not again until the thousand years were finished. This is the **first resurrection**.*

This great host will join the raptured saints and enter into millennial joys.

Satan shall be loosed at the end of the thousand years and shall deceive those who had never submitted their hearts to God, even in a nearly perfect environment. God destroys the rebellion and casts the Devil into the lake of fire where the beast (Antichrist) and False Prophet are.

Revelation 20:11-14 speaks of the **last resurrection**, the resurrection of the unbelieving dead and the Great White Throne Judgment.

> *And I saw a great white throne, and him that sat on it, from whose face the earth and the heaven fled away; and there was found no place for them. And I saw the dead, small and great, stand before God; and the books were opened: and another book was opened, which is the book of life: and the dead were judged out of those things which were written in the books, according to their works. And the sea gave up the dead which were in it; and death and hell delivered up the dead which were in them: and they were judged every man according to their works. And death and hell were cast into the lake of fire. This is the second death.*

At this juncture, God creates a new heaven and a new earth, wherein dwells only righteousness. Revelation 21:1, *"And I saw a new heaven and a new earth: for the first heaven and the first earth were passed away; and there was no more sea."*

The subject of biblical eschatology deserves a book by itself. But my plan is to deal with Islam and the end times. However, since the two eschatologies have so much in common, I thought it good first to give a quick review of Christian eschatology. Forgive the brevity. Some of the questions that may have been raised will be answered later.

CHAPTER TWO
THE COMING OF THE MAHDI

As we begin to study what Muslims believe about the end times, very quickly the vast difference between the teachings of the Koran and the Bible presents itself. The Bible begins with, "*God created the heavens and the earth*" (Genesis 1:1). It ends with God recreating a new heaven and a new earth for redeemed mankind. "*And I saw a new heaven and a new earth: for the first heaven and the first earth were passed away; and there was no more sea*" (Revelation 21:1). From the Fall in Genesis 3 till Revelation 22, the Bible chronologically reveals how God reconciled sinful man to Himself. The evidence for that was presented in Chapter One.

The Koran arranges itself by the length of the surahs (chapters), the longest surah first and the shortest surah last. There is no continuity of theme or thought. The Koran does not present a definite eschatology other than a Judgment Day when the righteous will be assigned to heaven and the unrighteous to hell. The eschatology of Islam comes via Hadith or traditions and quotes from Muslim scholars.

A summary of Islamic eschatology is as follows: Islamic eschatology is concerned with the Last Judgment. Like the other Abrahamic religions, Islam teaches the bodily resurrection of the dead, the fulfillment of a divine plan for creation, and the immortality of the human soul; the righteous are rewarded with the pleasures of heaven, while the unrighteous are punished in hell. A significant portion (about one third) of the Koran deals with these beliefs, with many portions of the Hadith elaborating on the themes and details. However, an elaborate set of beliefs have developed concerning the Mahdi, an Islamic messianic figure who is to be the savior and restorer of Islam.

SUNNI AND SHI'A

During the course of this book we will be referring to Shi'as and Sunnis, so it would be good to explain these terms. Both Sunni and Shi'a Muslims share the most fundamental Islamic beliefs and articles of faith. The differences between these two main sub-groups within Islam initially stemmed not from spiritual differences, but political ones. Over the centuries, however, these political differences have spawned a number of varying practices and positions which have come to carry a spiritual significance.

The division between Shi'a and Sunni dates back to the death of the Prophet Mohammed. The question of who was to take over the leadership of the Muslim nation caused the schism. Sunni Muslims agreed with the position taken by many of the Prophet's companions, that the new leader should be elected from among those capable of the job. This is what was done, and the Prophet Mohammed's close friend and advisor, Abu Bakr, became the first caliph of the Islamic nation. The word "Sunni" in Arabic comes from a word meaning "one who follows the traditions of the Prophet."

On the other hand, some Muslims shared the belief that leadership should have stayed within the Prophet's own family, among those specifically appointed by him, or among imams appointed by God Himself. The Shi'a Muslims believe that following the Prophet Mohammad's death, leadership should have passed directly to his cousin/son-in-law, Ali.

Ali challenged the leadership of Caliph Abu Bakr, resulting in a civil war in which Ali was killed. Throughout history, Shi'a Muslims have not recognized the authority of elected Muslim leaders, choosing instead to follow a line of imams which they believe have been appointed by the Prophet Mohammed or God Himself. The word "Shi'a" in Arabic means a group or supportive party of people.

The commonly known term is shortened from the historical "Shia-t-Ali," or "the Party of Ali." They are also known as followers of "Ahl-al-Bayt" or "People of the Household" (of the Prophet).[1]

TESTIMONY OF A ZEALOUS MUSLIM

You are about to read the words of a man of faith, faith in the final victory of Islam.

I'm writing this document as a response to requests from many Muslims and non-Muslims. I found many documents about this subject that contain a lot of false Hadeeths. This document is a result of a long research in evaluating every Hadeeth (true or false). The term "Mahdi" is a title meaning "The Guided one." Mahdi is a normal man who is going to follow the true Islam. His name will be Muhammad and his father's name will be 'Abdullah. He is a descendant from Ali and Fatima (daughter of the prophet Muhammad, pbuh – peace be upon him) so he will be descendant from al-Hasan or al-Husain. Mahdi will be very just and his capital will be Damascus. Allah told us that Jews will master the world two times (we live now in 1998 during the first one) and Mahdi will appear between those two periods and will rule through the last one. Mahdi is NOT a prophet but he is the final Rightly Guided Khalifa. Mahdi will lead Muslims to a great victory against the Christian Romans (i.e. all the white Europeans including the Americans). This great war is called al-Malhamah al-Kubrah or Armageddon. It will end up with a great victory to Muslims against Romans after six years. Muslims will take over their capital Rome (this can be any city). In the seventh year, the Antichrist will appear and a greater war will start between Jews and Muslims for 40 days (longer that usual days) and will end when Jesus (pbuh) will come and Muslims will kill all Jews. All people will convert into Islam. Peace will pervade the whole world. As Muslims, we should remember that the prophecy about Mahdi is one that will come to pass. This prophecy, however, does not absolve the Muslim *ummah* (community) from its duty to strive in the cause of Allah, oppose injustice, and seek peace and betterment of human condition. Centuries have passed from the time of the holy Prophet and there is a good possibility that many more will expire before the advent of the Mahdi. Muslims who are negligent in their duty hoping for a savior are committing a grave mistake and are not following the divine decrees ordained in Quran or taught by the Prophet Muhammad (pbuh).[2]

SIGNS OF THE COMING OF THE MAHDI

Most of the teachings about the end times come from the Hadith. The following are the main signs of the coming of the Mahdi. According to Moojan Momen, among the most commonly reported signs that presage the advent of the Mahdi in Shi'a Hadith are the following:

1. Before his coming will come the red death and the white death. The red death is the sword and the white death is plague.
2. Several figures will appear: the one-eyed Dajjal, and the Sufyani (an evil Muslim leader who opposes the Mahdi).
3. The Arabs will throw off the reins and take possession of their land, throwing out the authority of the foreigners.
4. There will be a great conflict in the land of Syria until it is destroyed.

5. Death and fear will afflict the people of Baghdad and Iraq. A fire will appear in the sky and a redness will cover them.[3]

GUIDED ONE

Who is the Mahdi? The term "MAHDI" is a title meaning "The Guided One." The main principle of the Mahdi is that he is a figure that is absolutely guided by God. This guidance is stronger than normal guidance, which usually involves a human being willfully acting according to the guidance of God. The Mahdi, on the other hand, has nothing of this human element, and his acts will be in complete accordance to God's will. According to scholar Moojan Momen, signs that Sunni and Shi'a are agreed upon include the following:

1. The Mahdi will be a descendant of Mohammed of the line of Fatima.
2. His name will be as the name of Mohammed.
3. He will rule for either seven, nine or nineteen years (though these years are consisted of days not necessarily the same as 24-hour days).
4. He will distribute wealth.
5. His coming will be accompanied by the raising of a Black Standard.
6. His coming will be accompanied by the appearance of the Dajjal (the "Great Deceiver").
7. There will be a lunar and solar eclipse within the same month of Ramadan.
8. A star with a luminous tail will rise from the East before the Mahdi emerges.
9. He will restore faith to its original form and eradicate moral corruption.

10. He will fight for the cause of Islam and make it prevail throughout the world.
11. He will have a broad forehead, a prominent nose, and his eyes will be naturally mascaraed.
12. He will fill the world with justice and fairness at a time when the world will be filled with oppression. [4]

SUNNI VIEW

The majority of Sunni Muslims do not consider the son of Hasan al-Askari to be the Mahdi nor to be in occultation (hiding). However, they do believe that the Madhi will come from Mohammad's family, more specifically from Al-Hasan's descendants. Sunnis believe that the Mahdi has not yet been born, and therefore his exact identity is only known to Allah. Aside from the Mahdi's precise genealogy, Sunnis accept many of the same Hadiths Shi'as accept about the predictions regarding the Mahdi's emergence, his acts, and his universal Khalifate. [5]

SHI'A VIEW

Muhammad al-Māhdī, also known as *Hujjat ibn al-Hasan* (born approximately July 29, 869 - unknown date), is the individual believed by Twelver Shī'a Muslims to be the Māhdī, the ultimate savior of humankind and the final Imām of the Twelve Imams. Twelver Shī'as believe that al-Māhdī was born in 869 and did not die but rather was hidden by God (this is referred to as the Occultation) and will later emerge with Jesus in order to fulfill their mission of bringing peace and justice to the world. He assumed the Imamate at 5 years of age. Sunnīs and other Shī'a schools do not consider ibn-al-Hasan to be the Māhdī. [6]

LINEAGE OF MOHAMMED

Several quotes show that the Mahdi will be a descendant of Mohammed. Hadhrat Abdullah bin Mas'ood says that Rasulullah (Mohammed) said, "This world will not come to an end until one person from my progeny does not rule over the Arabs, and his name will be the same as my name." Hadhrat Ali narrates that Rasulullah (Mohammed) said, "Even if only a day remains for Qiyamah (end of the world) to come, yet Allah will surely send a man from my family who will fill this world with such justice and fairness, just as it initially was filled with oppression."[7] From these quotes we learn that the Mahdi will be of the line of Mohammed and will be a ruler who will fill the world with justice and fairness.

MAHDI'S FEATURES AND CHARACTER

The sayings of the Hadith and the Hadhrats (Prophets) not only tell of the Mahdi's heritage and the nature of his rule, but also describe his features. Hadhrat Abu Saeed Khudri relates that Rasulullah (Mohammed) said, "Al Mahdi will be from my progeny. His forehead will be broad and his nose will be high. He will fill the world with justice and fairness at a time when the world will be filled with oppression. He will rule for seven years." Other Hadiths inform us that: he will be tall, he will be fair complexioned, his facial features will be similar to those of Rasulullah (Mohammed), his character will be exactly like that of Rasulullah (Mohammed), his father's name will be Abdullah, his mother's name will be Amina, he will speak with a slight stutter and occasionally this stutter will frustrate him, causing him to hit his hand upon his thigh. His age at the time of his emergence will be forty years. He will receive knowledge from Allah.[8]

A MUSLIM MILITARY LEADER

Several other important facts about the Mahdi emerge from the Hadiths. The Bani Kalb tribe will send an army to attack him (the Mahdi), only to be overpowered by the will of Allah. After the battle, Imam Mahdi will distribute the spoils of war. He will lead the people according to the Sunnat (Muslim traditions), and during his reign Islam will spread throughout the world. He will remain for seven years (after his emergence). He will pass away and the Muslims will perform his Janazah salaat (funeral). [9]

From this, we glean the fact that the Mahdi is a military man with an army. Like Mohammed, he will distribute the spoils of war with his soldiers. Leading the people according to Sunnat implies he will be a true Muslim and will follow all the traditions. His rule will result in Islam's conquest of the world. The Mahdi's death comes after a seven-year reign.

MIRACLE IN THE SKY

Another very interesting event is recorded. While the people will be pledging their allegiance to Imam Mahdi, a voice from the unseen will call out: "This is the representative of Allah, The Mahdi, listen to him and obey him." This announcement, which will be heard by all those present, will establish his authenticity. Another sign which will indicate the authenticity of Imam Mahdi will be that in the Ramadan prior to his emergence, an eclipse of the sun and moon will occur.[10] The incident is very similar to what we see at the baptism of Jesus.

> *And Jesus, when he was baptized, went up straightway out of the water: and, lo, the heavens were opened unto him, and he saw the Spirit of God descending like a dove, and lighting upon him: And lo a voice from heaven, saying, This is my*

beloved Son, in whom I am well pleased. (Matthew 3:16)

COVENANT MAKER

Hadhrat Abu Umamah says that Rasulullah (Mohammed) said: "There will be four peace agreements between you and the Romans. The fourth agreement will be mediated through a person who will be from the progeny of Hadhrat Haroon (Aaron) and will be upheld for seven years." This quote signifies that the Mahdi will make four covenants with the Romans. Joel Richardson in *The Islamic Antichrist* makes this comment: "While there is more than one tradition regarding the nature and timing of the Mahdi's ascendancy to power, one particular Hadith places the events at the final peace agreement between the Arabs and the Romans (Romans refer to Christians or, more generally, the West.) Although the peace agreement is made with the Romans, it is presumably mediated through a Jew from the priestly lineage of Aaron. The peace agreement will be made for seven years."[11]

RIDER ON A WHITE HORSE

Even though Muslims believe our Bible is corrupted, they claim that some portions of the "original" inspired books remain within the "corrupted" Bible. The tradition of extracting Judeo-Christian traditions is called *isra'iliyyat*. Muslim scholar Ka'b-Ahbar views the rider on the white horse in Revelation 6:2 as indeed the Mahdi. "*And I saw, and behold a white horse: and he that sat on him had a bow; and a crown was given unto him: and he went forth conquering, and to conquer.*" Two Egyptian authors in their book, *Al-Mahdi and the End Times*, quote him approvingly as follows:

I find the Mahdi recorded in the book of the Prophets....
For instance, the book of Revelation says, "And I saw and
beheld a white horse. He that sat on him...went forth
conquering and to conquer." It is clear that this man is
the Mahdi who will ride the white horse and judge by the
Qur'an (with justice) and with whom will be men with
marks of prostration on their foreheads (marks on their
foreheads from bowing in prayer with their head to the
ground five times daily).[12]

ARMY WITH BLACK FLAGS

During the time of the Mahdi, tradition tells of an army with black flags coming from Khurasan. Khurasan is an historical realm comprising a vast territory now lying in northeastern Iran, southern Turkmenistan and northern Afghanistan. Rasulullah (Mohammed) is quoted as saying, "When you see black flags approaching from Khurasan, then proceed towards it, for verily the Khalifa of Allah (the Mahdi) will be amongst it."[13] Another narration states: "The Messenger of Allah said: The black banners will come from the East and their hearts will be as firm as iron. Whoever hears of them should join them and give allegiance. Go towards it (the black flags) even if it means crawling upon snow."[14] The army with the black flags is unstoppable and conquers all its foes.

CONQUEST OF ISRAEL

In war after war, Israel has defeated the Muslim hordes that have endeavored to wipe it off the face of the earth and drive it into the sea. According to Muslim tradition, the Mahdi will lead this army of black flags and will conquer Israel for Islam. The Muslims will slaughter Jews until few remain and the Mahdi will set his headquarters in Jerusalem on the Temple Mount. Rasulullah (Mohammed) said: "Armies carrying black flags will come from Khurasan. No power will be able to stop them and they will finally reach Eela [Baitul Maqdas in Jerusalem] where they will erect their flags."[15] Note that Baitul Maqdas means "the holy house," referring to the Temple Mount in Jerusalem. The authors of the *Al Mahdi and the End of Time* comment on the conquest as follows:

> The Mahdi will be victorious and eradicate those pigs and dogs and the idols of this time so there will once more be a caliphate based on prophethood as the hadith states… Jerusalem will be the location of the rightly guided caliphate and the center of Islamic rule, which will be headed by Imam al-Mahdi…That will abolish the leadership of the Jews…and put an end to the domination of Satans who spit evil into people and cause corruption in the earth, making them slaves of false idols and ruling the world by laws other than the Shari'a [Islamic law] of the Lord of the worlds.[16]

Another famous tradition tells of even the rocks and trees fighting against the Jews:

> The Prophet said…the last hour would not come unless the Muslims will fight against the Jews and the Muslims would kill them until the Jews would hide themselves behind a stone or a tree and a stone or a tree would say: Muslim, or the servant of Allah, there is a Jew behind me; come and kill him.[17]

MIRACULOUS PROVIDER

Even though the Mahdi is only a man, he will have control over rain, wind and crops. The conditions would be similar to the Millennium, where peace and plenty abound. Mohammed reportedly said:

> *In the last days of ummah (universal Islamic community), the Mahdi will appear. Allah will give him power over the wind and the rain and the earth will bring forth its foliage. He will give away wealth profusely, flocks will be in abundance and the ummah will be large and honored…"*[18] *"In those years my community will enjoy a time of happiness such as they have never experienced before. Heaven will send rain upon them in torrents, the earth will not withhold any of its plants, and wealth will be available to all. A man will stand and say, "Give to me, Mahdi," and he will say, "Take."*[19]

THE ARCHAEOLOGIST

There are many more traditions, but let me mention just one more. Several traditions speak of the Mahdi being guided to Antioch and there discovering some previously undiscovered Bible scrolls and then the Ark of the Covenant from the Sea of Galilee. Ka'b Ahbar says, "He will be called "Mahdi" because he will guide to something hidden and will bring out the Torah and Gospel from a town called Antioch."[20] Ad-Dani said that he is called the Mahdi because he will be guided to a mountain in Syria from which he will bring forth the volumes of the Torah with which to argue against the Jews, and at his hands a group of them will become Muslims."[21] It seems the purpose of these archaeological finds is to bring forth new evidence with which to convince the Jews of the truth of Islam and the error of Judaism.

Joel Richardson in his book, *The Islamic Antichrist*, sums up the traditions of Islam concerning the Mahdi in twenty-one statements.

1. The Mahdi is Islam's primary messiah figure.
2. He will be a descendant of Mohammed and will bear Mohammed's name (Mohammed bin Abdullah).
3. He will be a very devout Muslim.
4. He will be an unparalleled spiritual, political and military world leader.
5. He will emerge after a period of great turmoil and suffering upon the earth.
6. He will establish justice and righteousness throughout the world and eradicate tyranny and oppression.
7. He will be the *caliph* and *imam* (vice regent and leader) of Muslims worldwide.
8. He will lead a world revolution and establish a new world order.
9. He will lead military action against all those who oppose him.
10. He will invade many countries.
11. He will make a seven-year treaty with a Jew of priestly lineage.
12. He will conquer Israel for Islam and lead the "faithful Muslims" in a final slaughter/battle against Jews.
13. He will establish the new Islamic world headquarters from Jerusalem.
14. He will rule for seven years (possibly as many as eight or nine).
15. He will cause Islam to be the only religion practiced on the earth.
16. He will appear riding a white horse (possibly symbolic).
17. He will discover some previously undiscovered biblical manuscripts that he will use to argue with the Jews and cause some Jews to convert to Islam.
18. He will also discover the Ark of the Covenant from the

Sea of Galilee, which he will bring to Jerusalem.
19. He will have supernatural power from Allah over the wind and the rain and the crops.
20. He will possess and distribute enormous amounts of wealth.
21. He will be loved by all the people.[22]

Just as Bible-believing Christians are looking for the blessed hope, the return of our Lord Jesus Christ to rapture His church, so Muslims worldwide are looking for the Mahdi to usher in the rule of Islam. There really cannot be two messiahs, one Christian and one Muslim. One will be true; the other will be false. In our next chapter we will see some amazing similarities between the Muslim Mahdi and the Biblical Antichrist.

CHAPTER THREE
IDENTIFYING THE ANTICHRIST

Seemingly intelligent people make unwise choices. Identifying the Antichrist is an unwise choice. Therefore, to identify the Antichrist is *not* the purpose of this chapter. Down through the history of the church, there have been Bible teachers predicting who the Antichrist would be. Every time they have been wrong. Mussolini, Hitler, Stalin, Gorbachev, John Fitzgerald Kennedy and, latest of all, Barack Husain Obama are just a few who have had the dubious honor of being named as the Antichrist.

Thus, it would be good to give an overview of what the Bible says about the Antichrist. The **Antichrist** is one who fulfills Biblical prophecies concerning an adversary of Christ while resembling him in a deceptive manner. "Antichrist" is the English translation of the original Koine Greek ἀντίκριστος, pronounced än-tē'-khrē-stos. It is made up of two root words, αντί + Χριστός (anti + Christos). "Αντί" can mean not only "against" and "opposite of," but also "in place of." "Χριστός," translated "Christ," is Greek for the Hebrew "Messiah" meaning "anointed," and refers to Jesus of Nazareth within Christian theology. The term "antichrist" appears 5 times in 1 John and 2 John of the New Testament – once in plural form and four times in the singular.[1]

1 John chapter 2 refers to many antichrists present at the time, while warning of one Antichrist who is coming. 1 John 2:18, *"Little children, it is the last time: and as ye have heard that antichrist shall come, even now are there many antichrists; whereby we know that it is the last time."* The "many antichrists" belong to the same spirit as that of the one Antichrist. John wrote that such antichrists deny "that Jesus is the Christ," "the Father and the Son," and would "not

confess that Jesus came in the flesh." Likewise, the one Antichrist denies the Father and the Son. 1 John 2:22, "*Who is a liar but he that denieth that Jesus is the Christ? He is antichrist, that denieth the Father and the Son.*"

This Antichrist mentioned by John is spoken of in more detail by Paul in 2 Thessalonians 2:3,4:

> *Let no man deceive you by any means: for that day shall not come, except there come a falling away first, and that man of sin be revealed, the son of perdition; Who opposeth and exalteth himself above all that is called God, or that is worshipped; so that he as God sitteth in the temple of God, shewing himself that he is God.*

Then in 2 Thessalonians 2:7-10 Paul sheds more light on the character of the Antichrist and his final demise.

> *For the mystery of iniquity doth already work: only he (the Holy Spirit) who now letteth will let, until he be taken out of the way. And then shall that Wicked be revealed, whom the Lord shall consume with the spirit of his mouth, and shall destroy with the brightness of his coming: Even him, whose coming is after the working of Satan with all power and signs and lying wonders, And with all deceivableness of unrighteousness in them that perish; because they received not the love of the truth, that they might be saved.*

ANTICHRIST IS ON THE HORIZON

Those of us who believe the Bible and take it seriously find the Antichrist and his work in various places, both in the Old and New Testaments. Before we see how the Antichrist relates to Islam, it will be good to study and understand the Biblical teachings concerning the Antichrist. He is all of the following:

> Unsurpassed political and military leader. (Revelation 13:4)
>
> Spiritual leader of the whole world. (Revelation 13:4)
>
> Makes a peace treaty with the Jews. (Daniel 9:27)
>
> Breaks the peace treaty. (Daniel 11:3)
>
> Systematically exterminates Jews and Christians. (Revelation 13:7 and 20:4)
>
> Captures and controls Jerusalem. (Zechariah 14:2)
>
> Changes times and laws. (Daniel 7:25)
>
> Blasphemes God and sets himself up as God. (2 Thessalonians 2:4)
>
> Works in league with Satan and the False Prophet. (Revelation 14:11-18)
>
> Is destroyed by God and cast into the bottomless pit. (Revelation 20:10)

All of the above are clearly revealed in the Bible. They are not the imaginings of some fanatic; not a fanciful scheme of interpretation derived by men. As we compare scripture with scripture, a scenario presents itself which will surely unfold in the days and years that lie ahead.

MAN OF PEACE

As time passes, we can expect conditions to continue to deteriorate. America, long the world's strongest financial bastion, suffers from unwise spending and borrowing. Seemingly, there is no hope of reversal. More than likely, inflation and its concomitant woes will only increase. Jihad, Islam's 1,400 years' war to impose Muslim law (sharia) on the whole world, continues apace. Iran and Israel's standoff could explode at any time. Disruption of oil supplies from the Middle East could cause economic collapse in America. Expect chaos in Europe as Muslims continue to gain power by having more than five times as many babies as the Europeans.

Into the midst of this international turmoil rides a charismatic figure, the like of whom the world has never seen. The Bible describes him in Revelation 6:2, *"And I saw, and behold a white horse: and he that sat on him had a bow; and a crown was given unto him: and he went forth conquering, and to conquer."* The picture here is surely symbolic. Into the chaos comes a king, a leader, with a bow but no arrows! He conquers at this time, not by might of arms, but by cunning diplomacy and rhetoric.

John, in the Revelation of Jesus Christ, speaks of a beast rising out of the sea. Revelation 13:1, *"And I stood upon the sand of the sea, and saw a beast rise up out of the sea* (nations), *having seven heads and ten horns, and upon his horns ten crowns, and upon his heads the name of blasphemy."* Verses 4-8 give more details about this beast, which Daniel identifies as a king.

> *And they worshipped the dragon which gave power unto the beast: and they worshipped the beast, saying, Who is like unto the beast? who is able to make war with him? And there was given unto him a mouth speaking great things and blasphemies; and power was given unto him to continue forty and two months. And he opened his mouth in blasphemy against*

God, to blaspheme his name, and his tabernacle, and them that dwell in heaven. And it was given unto him to make war with the saints, and to overcome them: and power was given him over all kindreds, and tongues, and nations. And all that dwell upon the earth shall worship him, whose names are not written in the book of life of the Lamb slain from the foundation of the world.

In seeking to understand scripture, it is best to let scripture interpret itself. Who is the dragon referred to in verse four? Revelation 12:9 leaves no doubt as to his identity: *"And the great dragon was cast out, that old serpent, called the Devil, and Satan, which deceiveth the whole world: he was cast out into the earth, and his angels were cast out with him."* We now learn there is a connection between Satan and the Antichrist. Satan empowers this human leader with supernatural skills and powers. World governments surrender to his charms and promises with the exclamation, "Who is able to make war with him?"

COVENANT MAKER AND BREAKER

Daniel writes of the Antichrist signing a covenant (peace treaty) with Israel for seven years. Daniel 9:27,

And he shall confirm the covenant with many for one week (a week is equal to seven years) and in the midst of the week (three and one - half years) he shall cause the sacrifice and the oblation to cease, and for the overspreading of abominations he shall make it desolate, even until the consummation, and that determined shall be poured upon the desolate.

Again in Daniel 11:31,

… and they shall pollute the sanctuary of strength, (the rebuilt Jewish temple) and shall take away the daily sacrifice, and they shall place the abomination that maketh desolate." and Daniel 12:11, *"And from the time that the daily sacrifice shall be taken away, and the abomination that maketh desolate set up, there shall be a thousand two hundred and ninety days.*

In Matthew 24:15 Jesus corroborates these prophecies of Daniel. *"When ye therefore shall see the abomination of desolation, spoken of by Daniel the prophet, stand in the holy place, (whoso readeth, let him understand:)"* and Mark 13:14, *"But when ye shall see the abomination of desolation, spoken of by Daniel the prophet, standing where it ought not, (let him that readeth understand,) then let them that be in Judaea flee to the mountains:)"*

ANOTHER HOLOCAUST IS COMING

After revoking his covenant with the Jews, Antichrist institutes a program for exterminating both Jews and Tribulation saints. Revelation 20:4,

And I saw thrones, and they sat upon them, and judgment was given unto them: and I saw the souls of them that were beheaded for the witness of Jesus, and for the word of God, and which had not worshipped the beast, neither his image, neither had received his mark upon their foreheads, or in their hands; and they lived and reigned with Christ a thousand years.

In Revelation 7:9,13,14,

After this I beheld, and, lo, a great multitude, which no man could number, of all nations, and kindreds, and people, and

tongues, stood before the throne, and before the Lamb, clothed with white robes, and palms in their hands; And one of the elders answered, saying unto me, What are these which are arrayed in white robes? and whence came they? And I said unto him, Sir, thou knowest. And he said to me, These are they which came out of great tribulation, and have washed their robes, and made them white in the blood of the Lamb.

Yes, according to God's Word, hard times lie ahead for the true people of God.

CHANGES TIMES AND LAWS

During the last presidential election campaign, the word "change" was prominent. More changes than this world dreams of are coming in the future. Daniel 7:25,

And he shall speak great words against the most High, and shall wear out the saints of the most High, and think to change times and laws: and they shall be given into his hand until a time(one year) and times(two years) and the dividing of time (one-half year).

Again we see the time line of three and one-half years. During this time the Antichrist will blaspheme the God of heaven. Paul, in 2 Thessalonians 3:2, speaks directly of this: "*Who opposeth and exalteth himself above all that is called God, or that is worshipped; so that he as God sitteth in the temple of God, shewing himself that he is God.*" The Antichrist and his False Prophet wreak havoc among the people of God.

This wearing out of the saints is addressed in Revelation 13:11-18. "*And I beheld another beast coming up out of the earth; and he had two horns like a lamb, and he spake as a dragon.*" We are now introduced to the False Prophet who will promote Antichrist's religion and wage all-out war against all who will not submit. Verse 12, *"And he exerciseth all the power of the first beast before him, and causeth the earth and them which dwell therein to worship the first beast..."* Satan, ever since his rebellion against God, has had grandiose plans to replace God with himself.

Now we see the unholy trinity: the dragon, Satan; the Antichrist, ruling the whole world with an iron fist, and the False Prophet, the religious leader who enforces worship of the Antichrist. In the process they will change the calendar so as not to read B.C. or A.D. They will certainly do away with Sunday, which in days gone by was almost universally set aside as the day to worship God and to rest. The laws of the land based on Jude-Christian ethics will go by the board.

ANTICHRIST HATRED OF ISRAEL

Down through the centuries, Satan has used individuals to seek to destroy Israel. Pharaoh brought them into captivity and destroyed all the male babies (except Moses, whom God protected miraculously). Haman hatched a devilish plan to eradicate the Jews once and for all. Herod massacred all Jew babies two years old and younger in the environs of Bethlehem. Hitler, with his "final solution," killed six million Jews.

Revelation tells us about the Antichrist's effort to destroy Israel. Revelation 12:1, *"And there appeared a great wonder in heaven; a woman clothed with the sun, and the moon under her feet, and upon her head a crown of twelve stars."* The woman, of course, is Israel, and the twelve stars refer to the twelve tribes. Revelation 12:2-5 describes Antichrist's attempt to destroy the infant Jesus and his failure to do so.

And she being with child cried, travailing in birth, and

pained to be delivered. And there appeared another wonder in heaven; and behold a great red dragon, having seven heads and ten horns, and seven crowns upon his heads… and the dragon stood before the woman which was ready to be delivered, for to devour her child as soon as it was born. And she brought forth a man child, who was to rule all nations with a rod of iron: and her child was caught up unto God, and to his throne.

Verses 13-16 give us more details of Israel's deliverance.

And when the dragon saw that he was cast unto the earth, he persecuted the woman which brought forth the man child. And to the woman were given two wings of a great eagle, that she might fly into the wilderness, into her place, where she is nourished for a time, and times, and half a time, from the face of the serpent. And the serpent cast out of his mouth water as a flood after the woman, that he might cause her to be carried away of the flood. And the earth helped the woman, and the earth opened her mouth, and swallowed up the flood which the dragon cast out of his mouth.

The mention of time, times, and half a time date this event. It is during the Great Tribulation, the last three and one-half years of Antichrist's reign. This providential rescue saves Israel from extinction. Revelation 13:5-7 sums up Antichrist's rage against God and His people.

And there was given unto him a mouth speaking great things and blasphemies; and power was given unto him to continue forty and two months. And he opened his mouth in blasphemy against God, to blaspheme his name, and his tabernacle, and them that dwell in heaven. And it was given unto him to make war with the saints, and to overcome them: and power was given him over all kindreds, and tongues, and nations.

ANTICHRIST'S CAPTURE OF JERUSALEM

Two references from the Old Testament show that Antichrist will conquer Jerusalem and set up his headquarters there. Zechariah 14:2,

> *For I will gather all nations against Jerusalem to battle; and the city shall be taken, and the houses rifled, and the women ravished; and half of the city shall go forth into captivity, and the residue of the people shall not be cut off from the city.*

The people who were not cut off were those who submitted to Antichrist's rule.

Ezekiel also foretells the conquest of Jerusalem by Gog, another name for Antichrist. Ezekiel 38:9-12.

> *Thou shalt ascend and come like a storm, thou shalt be like a cloud to cover the land, thou, and all thy bands, and many people with thee. Thus saith the Lord GOD; It shall also come to pass, that at the same time shall things come into thy mind, and thou shalt think an evil thought: And thou shalt say, I will go up to the land of unwalled villages; I will go to them that are at rest, that dwell safely, all of them dwelling without walls, and having neither bars nor gates, To take a spoil, and to take a prey; to turn thine hand upon the desolate places that are now inhabited, and upon the people that are gathered out of the nations, which have gotten cattle and goods, that dwell in the midst of the land* (in the center of the world).

Israel, having made a peace treaty with the Antichrist, has given up its arms. Its people live in unwalled villages and are at rest. Before the restoration of Israel as a nation in 1948, it was a desolate land. Now Palestine has been repopulated by people (Jews) from many nations, and has experienced outstanding prosperity. Jerusalem is the geographical center of planet earth. Gog sets his sight upon Israel and captures it for himself.

ANTICHRIST'S DEMISE

Antichrist has a famous beginning but an infamous ending. Several verses tell of God's ultimate victory over the unholy trinity. 2 Thessalonians 2:8, 9,

And then shall that Wicked be revealed, whom the Lord shall consume with the spirit of his mouth, and shall destroy with the brightness of his coming: Even him, whose coming is after the working of Satan with all power and signs and lying wonders.

Daniel speaks very clearly of Antichrist's demise. Daniel 7:8-11,

I considered the horns, and, behold, there came up among them another little horn (the Antichrist), before whom there were three of the first horns plucked up by the roots: and, behold, in this horn were eyes like the eyes of man, and a mouth speaking great things. I beheld till the thrones were cast down, and the Ancient of days (Jesus Christ) did sit, whose garment was white as snow, and the hair of his head like the pure wool: his throne was like the fiery flame, and his wheels as burning fire. A fiery stream issued and came forth from before him: thousand thousands ministered unto him, and ten thousand times ten thousand stood before him: the judgment was set, and the books were opened. I beheld then because of the voice of the great words which the horn spake: I beheld even till the beast was slain, and his body destroyed, and given to the burning flame.

Revelation 19:19,20 describes the results of the final battle.

And I saw the beast, and the kings of the earth, and their armies, gathered together to make war against him that sat on the horse, and against his army. And the beast was taken, and with him the false prophet that wrought miracles before him, with which he deceived them that had received the mark of the beast, and them that worshipped his image. These both were cast alive into a lake of fire burning with brimstone.

LAST BATTLE

The beast (Antichrist) and the False Prophet are now in the lake of fire. Revelation 20 explodes with startling facts. First, Satan is thrown into the bottomless pit, to be bound for a thousand years. Verses 1-3,

And I saw an angel come down from heaven, having the key of the bottomless pit and a great chain in his hand. And he laid hold on the dragon, that old serpent, which is the Devil, and Satan, and bound him a thousand years, And cast him into the bottomless pit, and shut him up, and set a seal upon him, that he should deceive the nations no more, till the thousand years should be fulfilled: and after that he must be loosed a little season.

Next, comes the resurrection of those martyred by the Antichrist. Verses 4-5,

> *And I saw thrones, and they sat upon them, and judgment was given unto them: and I saw the souls of them that were beheaded for the witness of Jesus, and for the word of God, and which had not worshipped the beast, neither his image, neither had received his mark upon their foreheads, or in their hands; and they lived and reigned with Christ a thousand years. But the rest of the dead lived not again until the thousand years were finished. This is the first resurrection.*

Note that the believers in Christ have been raptured by Christ before the Great Tribulation.

Revelation 19:11-14 gives more details of the final battle between Christ and Antichrist. One of those facts is that the raptured church will be with Christ in that final battle.

> *And I saw heaven opened, and behold a white horse; and he that sat upon him was called Faithful and True, and in righteousness he doth judge and make war. His eyes were as a flame of fire, and on his head were many crowns; and he had a name written, that no man knew, but he himself. And he was clothed with a vesture dipped in blood: and his name is called The Word of God. And the armies which were in heaven followed him upon white horses, clothed in fine linen, white and clean.*

The armies clothed in fine linen are those who have been judged at the Judgment Seat of Christ (2 Corinthians 5:10) and are now forevermore with the Lord.

Revelation 20:5 mentions the Millennium for the first time. There will be a thousand years of peace. *"But the rest of the dead lived not again until the thousand years were finished. This is the first resurrection."* Verse 6 teaches that the resurrected saints shall be priests of God and of Christ and shall reign with him a thousand years. *"Blessed and holy is he that hath part in the first resurrection: on such the second death hath no power, but they shall be priests of God and of Christ, and shall reign with him a thousand years."*

At the close of the thousand years, Satan will be loosed for a season to test those who lived during that time. Multitudes that enjoyed God's entire blessing during the Millennium rebel against God and choose to follow the devil. Revelation 20:7-10 record the last battle. *And when the thousand years are expired, Satan shall be loosed out of his prison, And shall go out to deceive the nations which are in the four quarters of the earth, Gog and Magog, to gather them together to battle*: the number of whom is as the sand of the sea.

And they went up on the breadth of the earth, and compassed the camp of the saints about, and the beloved city: and fire came down from God out of heaven, and devoured them. And the devil that deceived them was cast into the lake of fire and brimstone, where the beast and the false prophet are, and shall be tormented day and night for ever and ever.

Now that the enemies of God are put away there comes the Great White Throne judgment where the unsaved will be judged. Then God recreates and brings into being a new heaven and a new earth wherein dwells righteousness.

This, my friend, is not wishful thinking but the revealed Word of God. God is directing all things after the counsel of His will, and His will shall be done on earth as it is heaven.

CHAPTER FOUR
THE MAHDI AND THE ANTICHRIST

In Chapter Two we studied what the Hadith (Muslim traditions) teach about the Mahdi, (the guided one) the Islamic Messiah, the twelfth imam, the last caliph, leader of worldwide Islam. Then in Chapter Three we studied what the Bible teaches about the Antichrist, the imposter who usurps for himself worldwide dominion and sets himself up as the God of forces.

In this and following chapters we are going to see amazing similarities between the Mahdi of Islam and the Antichrist of Biblical Christianity. I am indebted to Walid Shoebat, a former Palestinian Muslim terrorist, who has accepted Jesus Christ as his Savior and Lord and the Bible as his authority. His book, *God's War on Terror – Islam, Prophecy and the Bible,* will reward anyone who will read it.

BOTH ANTICHRIST AND THE MAHDI DENY THE TRINITY

Anyone who deals with Muslims knows that they are greatly offended by the concept of God being a trinity. The Koran speaks clearly on the subject: *"They blaspheme who say that Allah is the third of three"* (Surah 5:73). To Muslims, Allah is an indivisible unit.

In the Bible, God has revealed Himself as a tri-unity, i.e., one substance or essence, existing in three distinct persons. A verse in the Old Testament very clearly presents our God as a trinity, i.e., three distinct persons in the Godhead. Isaiah 48:16, *"Come ye near unto me, hear ye this; I have not spoken in secret from the beginning; from the time that it was, there **am I**: and now the **Lord GOD**, and his **Spirit**, hath sent me."* In this verse Jesus Christ, the sent One, reveals it was the Lord God (Father) and His Holy Spirit that had sent Him.

Again, at the baptism of Jesus, the trinity is clearly seen. Matthew 3:16,

> *And Jesus, when he was baptized, went up straightway out of the water: and, lo, the heavens were opened unto him, and he saw the Spirit of God descending like a dove, and lighting upon him: And lo a voice from heaven, saying, This is my beloved Son, in whom I am well pleased.*

The Son was in the baptismal waters, the Father speaks from heaven, and the Holy Spirit descends as a dove. A remarkable display of the trinity indeed!

John, in his first epistle, reveals that Antichrist denies the trinity by denying the Father and the Son. 1 John 2:22, "*Who is a liar but he that denieth that Jesus is the Christ? He is **antichrist**, that denieth the Father and the Son.*" Then the Mahdi, being a defender of the Koran and traditional Islam, will deny the doctrine of the trinity. So the first similarity between Antichrist and the Mahdi is that they both deny the trinity as revealed in the Bible.

Although the Muslims deny the trinity, Mohammed, for all practical purposes, is put on a level with deity. In their *Shahadatan* (confession), "There is no god but Allah and Mohammed is His messenger." Shoebat comments,

> Nowhere in the Bible do we see an attempt to so elevate a prophet by placing him side by side with God in creedal form. It is unimaginable to think of a creed that demands, let's say, "There is no god but Allah and Ezekiel is his messenger." Why so much emphasis on one particular prophet? Why would not the Muslim insist that Mohammed is one of Allah's messengers? But the messenger! That makes him more important than Jesus Christ Himself! Why would

Mohammed allow himself to be so elevated – even above Jesus Himself?[1]

Good question.

BOTH ANTICHRIST AND THE MAHDI DENY THE FATHER AND THE SON

John is very specific as he identifies the Antichrist as one who denies the Son and the Father. Later in his first epistle John has more to say about Antichrist. 1 John 4:2, 3,

> *Hereby know ye the Spirit of God: Every spirit that confesseth that Jesus Christ is come in the flesh is of God: And every spirit that confesseth not that Jesus Christ is come in the flesh is not of God: and this is that spirit of antichrist, whereof ye have heard that it should come; and even now already is it in the world.*

The phrase **come in the flesh** refers to the incarnation of Jesus Christ. John 1:14, *"And the Word* (God) *was made flesh, and dwelt among us, (and we beheld his glory, the glory as of the only begotten of the Father,) full of grace and truth."*

Islam vehemently denies the incarnation of Jesus Christ and, as such, is the spirit of Antichrist. Not only does the Koran deny the trinity; it also denies the deity of Jesus Christ. Surah 4:171,

> *O followers of the Book! do not exceed the limits in your religion, and do not speak (lies) against Allah, but (speak) the truth; the Messiah, Isa son of Marium is only an apostle of Allah and His Word which He communicated to Marium and a spirit from Him; believe therefore in Allah and His apostles, and say not, Three. Desist, it is better for you; Allah is only*

one God; far be It from His glory that He should have a son, whatever is in the heavens and whatever is in the earth is His, and Allah is sufficient for a Protector.

Muslims say many nice things about Isa (Jesus) and some even say they love Jesus more than the Christians do! For instance, they believe in the virgin birth. Surah 3:45-47,

When the angels said: O Marium, surely Allah gives you good news with a Word from Him (of one) whose name is the Messiah, Isa son of Marium, worthy of regard in this world and the hereafter and of those who are made near (to Allah). And he shall speak to the people when in the cradle and when of old age, and (he shall be) one of the good ones. She said: My Lord! when shall there be a son (born) to me, **and man has not touched me?** *He said: Even so, Allah creates what He pleases; when He has decreed a matter, He only says to it, Be, and it is.*

They believe that Jesus is sinless. They refer to Him as the Messiah, the word of Allah, and the spirit of Allah. Underneath this façade of honoring Jesus, though, is the fact that they deny His incarnation, His deity, His death on the cross, and His resurrection (for if He did not die, He cannot arise from the dead). Their Jesus who comes back to earth will be a fanatical Muslim who helps the Mahdi exterminate Jews and Tribulation saints. In fact, as we will see later in our study, the Jesus of the Koran has no resemblance to the Jesus of the Bible.

BOTH ANTICHRIST AND THE MAHDI DENY THE DEITY OF CHRIST

Islam holds to the strictest form of monotheism, i.e., the absolute oneness of God. They refer to this doctrine as *tawhid*. Since this is one of the essential tenets of Islam, it is a most serious sin to deny it. The sin of alleging that Allah has a partner is called *shirk*. No sin imaginable can be compared to it. Just as committing the unpardonable sin of rejecting Jesus Christ as Lord and Savior, so believing that Allah has a partner (Son) is the unpardonable sin of Islam. "If a person dies (committing the sin of shirk and never repents of it), he will be a permanent resident in hell-fire."[2]

Several surahs comment on the Muslim tenet that Christ is not the Son of God. For example, Surah 19:89-91 says,

> *And they say: The Beneficent God has taken (to Himself) a son. Certainly you have made an abominable assertion. The heavens may almost be rent thereat, and the earth cleave asunder, and the mountains fall down in pieces, That they ascribe a son to the Beneficent God.*

BOTH ANTICHRIST AND THE MAHDI DENY THE CROSS

Islam denies the three cardinal doctrines of Christianity: the incarnation of Jesus Christ, His death on the cross, and His resurrection from the grave. Surah 4:157,158,

> *And their saying: Surely we have killed the Messiah, Isa son of Marium, the apostle of Allah; and* **they did not kill him** *nor did they crucify him, but it appeared to them so (like Isa) and most surely those who differ therein are only in a doubt about it; they have no knowledge respecting it, but only follow a conjecture, and they killed him not for sure.*

Muslims are at odds at what happened at the cross. Some say Judas Iscariot was made to look like Jesus and thus it was Judas who died, not Jesus. Amid their conjecture of what happened one thing is sure: they affirm that Jesus Christ did not die on the cross, but was caught up to heaven by Allah without dying.

It is amazing how Islam has targeted Christianity. To believe our cardinal doctrines make us anathema (cursed) to the Muslim and destined to be a permanent resident of hell-fire. Both Mohammed and the Mahdi, who is yet to be revealed, personify the antichrist spirit of a hatred and denial of all that we believe and call sacred.

BOTH ANTICHRIST AND THE MAHDI ARE DECEIVERS

Satan enters the Garden of Eden and summarily deceives Eve into rebelling against God, her Creator. Genesis 3:13, *And the LORD God said unto the woman, What is this that thou hast done? And the woman said, The serpent beguiled* (deceived*) me, and I did eat."* John once again describes Antichrist as one who deceives. 2 John 1:7, *"For many deceivers are entered into the world, who confess not that Jesus Christ is come in the flesh. This is a deceiver and an **antichrist**."* Paul points out that the Antichrist, the man of sin, the son of perdition will be a deceiver. 2 Thessalonians 2:9,

> *Even him, whose coming is after the working of Satan with all power and signs and lying wonders, And with all **deceivableness** of unrighteousness in them that perish; because they received not the love of the truth, that they might be saved.*

No doubt about it. The Antichrist will be an ace at deception.

But what about the Mahdi and the Islam he will represent? Would you believe that Allah in the Koran actually brags about being the world's greatest deceiver? We will let the Koran and Allah speak for themselves. Surah 3:54,

> *And they planned* (the word for planned is 'makara' in Arabic which means to deceive, scheme, connive) *and Allah (also) planned, and Allah is the best of planners."* Surah 8:30,

> *"And when those who disbelieved devised plans against you that they might confine you or slay you or drive you away; and they devised plans and Allah too had arranged a plan; and Allah is the best of planners."*

In the Bible, "deceiver," "schemer," and "liar" refer to Satan. Incredibly, in Islam and the Koran, these terms refer to Allah. For example, *makara,* as we have seen, in Arabic means to deceive, scheme, hatch up, connive. Allah names himself Khayrul-Makireen, the greatest of all deceivers.[3] Muslim teachers sanction the practice of lying and deceiving to further the cause of Islam. Abdullah Al-Ghazali, one of the most famous Muslim theologians of all time, sanctioned lying in this way.

Speaking is a means of achieving objectives. If a praiseworthy aim is attainable through both telling the truth and lying, it is unlawful to accomplish through lying because there is no need for it. When it is possible to achieve such an aim by lying but not telling the truth, it is permissible to lie if attaining the goal is permissible.[4]

BOTH ANTICHRIST AND THE MAHDI CLAIM TO BE MESSIAH

Jews, Christians, and Muslims are all looking for a Messiah. In each case he is expected to make wrongs right and usher in a time of peace and prosperity. "*Al-Mahdi* is "the rightly-guided one" who, according to Islamic Hadith (traditions), will come before the end of time to make the entire world Muslim."[5] The Jews are awaiting their Messiah, who they say is yet to come. When He comes, according to Jewish tradition, He will kill Satan Armilus, whom the Gentiles call the Antichrist, and usher in the Jewish kingdom. The Bible predicts that Christ, the Anointed, the Messiah, will come and defeat the Antichrist and set up His Millennial kingdom.

BOTH ANTICHRIST AND THE MAHDI WORK FALSE MIRACLES

The coming of Antichrist will be accompanied by signs and false wonders. Paul speaks of this in 2 Thessalonians 2:8,9,

> *And then shall that Wicked be revealed, whom the Lord shall consume with the spirit of his mouth, and shall destroy with the brightness of his coming: Even him, whose coming is after the working of Satan with **all power and signs and lying wonders**.*

Muslim traditions credit the Mahdi with remarkable powers. Mohammed reportedly said:

> *In the last days of ummah [universal Islamic community], the Mahdi will appear. Allah will give him power over the wind and the rain and the earth will bring forth its foliage. He will give away wealth profusely, flocks will be in abundance and the ummah will be large and honored...*[6]

BOTH ANTICHRIST AND THE MAHDI RIDE A WHITE HORSE

In our study of the coming of the Mahdi, we saw that Muslim authors see the Mahdi as the one riding the white horse in Revelation Chapter 6. Muslim scholar Ka'b-Ahbar views the rider on the white horse in Revelation 6:2 as indeed the Mahdi. "*And I saw, and behold a white horse: and he that sat on him had a bow; and a crown was given unto him: and he went forth conquering, and to conquer.*" Two Egyptian authors, in their book, *Al-Mahdi and the End*

of Time, quote him approvingly as follows:
> I find the Mahdi recorded in the book of the Prophets... For instance, the book of Revelation says, *"And I saw and beheld a white horse. He that sat on him...went forth conquering, and to conquer."* It is clear that this man is the Mahdi who will ride the white horse and judge by the Koran (with justice) and with whom will be men with marks of prostration on their foreheads [marks on their foreheads from bowing in prayer with their head to the ground five times daily]. [7]

The rider on the white horse fits the Antichrist: he rides as a king, he has a bow but no arrows, and following him are three more horses. The red horse represents war on the saints and massive killings by the sword. The black horse represents the famine that will accompany the plagues of the Tribulation Period. The pale horse represents death and hell that result from the wrath of God outpoured upon a wicked world. Certainly, the man on the white horse is the Antichrist.

BOTH ANTICHRIST AND THE MAHDI ATTEMPT TO CHANGE THE TIME AND LAWS

In our study of the Antichrist we learned that he would attempt to change the times and the laws. Daniel 7:25, *"And he shall speak great words against the most High, and shall wear out the saints of the most High, and think **to change times** and **laws**: and they shall be given into his hand until a time and times and the dividing of time."* The Mahdi will have a mandate to change both the laws and the time (calendar).

Islam's stated purpose is to bring the whole world under shariah law, i.e., the rule of the Koran. Islam has a judiciary peculiar to itself. Even in England and Canada today, Muslims are pushing to be judged by their own laws. The Muslims have their own calendar, and they impose their calendar on all the countries they control. Their calendar begins with the *Hijra,* Mohammed's flight to and conquest of Medina. It is considered a divine command to use a Hijra calendar (which employs lunar months). Years are designated in English A.H. or After Hijra.[8] The Muslim holy day is Friday. Sunday as a day of worship would be abolished.

BOTH ANTICHRIST AND THE MAHDI DENY WOMEN'S RIGHTS

Antichrist will not be a lover of women. Daniel 11:37, *"Neither shall he regard the God of his fathers, nor the **desire of women**, nor regard any god: for he shall magnify himself above all."* In other words women and what women want are not important in Antichrist's reign.

Former Roman Catholic nun Karen Armstrong converted to Islam and has become a champion for her newfound faith. She tells us that the emancipation of women was dear to the prophet's heart.[9] But a glance at the Koran and prevailing practice in Muslim nations dispel this idea. In Surah 2:228,

> *The men are a degree above them (women). Surah 2:282, "And call in to witness from among your men two witnesses; but if there are not two men, then one man and **two women** from among those whom you choose to be witnesses...*

In other words one man is equal to two women!

Saudi Arabia, the womb of Islam, has little concern for the desire of women. Some startling facts came to light in 2000 A.D.

> Women must not drive cars, and must not be driven, except by an employee, or husband, or close relative—and then must not occupy the front seat. The authorities monitor all gatherings of persons, especially women, and dis-

perse women found in public places such as restaurants. Women may study abroad, but only at the undergraduate level— if accompanied by a spouse or an immediate male relative.[10]

So much for the emancipation of women!

BOTH ANTICHRIST AND THE MAHDI RULE OVER TEN ENTITIES

There is no doubt the Antichrist will rule over ten kings. Revelation 17:12, 13 make it clear. *"And the ten horns which thou sawest are ten kings, which have received no kingdom as yet; but receive power as kings one hour with the beast. These have one mind, and shall give their power and strength unto the beast."*

Plans are under way for the coming caliphate. The caliphate is a worldwide Muslim government with a spiritual head called the caliph. In 2002, a *"Plan for the Return of the Caliphate"* was written by Abu Qanit al-Sharif al-Hasani. The plan calls for the caliph to be assisted by a ten-member council.[11] Is it not remarkable how these similarities continue to mount?

CHAPTER FIVE
THE MAHDI AND THE ANTICHRIST - CONTINUED

In our comparison of the Mahdi and the Antichrist, we have seen amazing similarities, but more are to come. Thus far, the striking similarities are: both deny the trinity, deny the Father and the Son, deny the deity of Christ, deny the cross, deny women's rights, claim to be the messiah, work false miracles, ride a white horse, are deceivers, attempt to change the times and laws, and rule over ten entities. Let us look at more similarities.

BOTH ANTICHRIST AND THE MAHDI ARE THE SOURCE OF DEATH AND WAR

The rider on the white horse in Revelation, chapter 6, is identified as the Antichrist by Biblical scholars. Similarly, the Hadith claims that the rider is the Mahdi. Revelation 6 presents four horses and horsemen. Following the white horse comes the red horse, i.e., war and bloodshed, specifically the blood of the saints. Revelation 20:4

> *And I saw thrones, and they sat upon them, and judgment was given unto them: and I saw the souls of them that were **beheaded** for the witness of Jesus, and for the word of God, and which had not worshipped the beast, neither his image, neither had received his mark upon their foreheads, or in their hands; and they lived and reigned with Christ a thousand years.*

This holocaust will make the French revolution with its hideous guillotine look like a church picnic! This time it will not be a guillotine, but a Muslim sword.

The fact that the Mahdi is a military commander appears frequently in the Hadith or Muslim traditions. This quote is an example:

> *The Mahdi will be a man of war who leads an army that Muslims call the Black Flags.* "*The Messenger of Allah said: The black banners (flags) will come from the East and their hearts will be as firm as iron. Whoever hears of them should join them and give allegiance. Go towards it (the black flags) even if it means crawling upon snow.*[1]

The army with the black flags is unstoppable and conquers all its foes.

Daniel 11:37,38 reveals the nature of this world leader.

> *Neither shall he regard the God of his fathers, nor the desire of women, nor regard any god: for he shall magnify himself above all. But in his estate shall he honour* **the God of forces**: *and a god whom his fathers knew not shall he honour with gold, and silver, and with precious stones, and pleasant things.*

Historically, Islamic armies have been famous for taking loot. The gold, silver, precious stones and pleasant things certainly speak of loot taken in military campaigns.

What term could more adequately describe the religion of Islam and its god, Allah, than the God of forces? From its inception until the present day, war and force have characterized Islam. Mohammed, during his lifetime, conquered all of Arabia for Islam. After his death, his followers spread war and death until they reigned from India in the east to Spain in the west. Islam stagnated in the 1400s, thus the rampage of war and death ceased. During this time (the fourteenth and fifteenth centuries) the Renaissance and the Reformation breathed new life into Europe. As a result, Muslims became the conquered instead of the conquerors.

But the oil wealth given to the Muslims (especially Saudi Arabia) by the work of American and European engineers, and the policy of Franklin Delano Roosevelt, enabled Islam to reassert itself on the world scene. The Brotherhood of Egypt used terrorist techniques against the British in the 1950s. The bombing of embassies in Africa and the Middle East, the bombing of railways in Spain and England, the infamous 9/11 bombings of the World Trade Center and many, many more – all carried out by Islamists – show that Islam honors the God of forces.

ANTICHRIST, A MAN OF WAR

Two references from the Old Testament show that Antichrist will be a man of war and one who honors the God of forces. Zechariah 14:2,

> *For I will gather all nations against Jerusalem to battle; and the city shall be taken, and the houses rifled, and the women ravished; and half of the city shall go forth into captivity, and the residue of the people shall not be cut off from the city.*

The people who were not cut off were those who submitted to Antichrist's rule.

Ezekiel also foretells the conquest of Jerusalem by Gog, another name for Antichrist. Ezekiel 38:9-12,

> *Thou shalt ascend and come like a storm, thou shalt be like a cloud to cover the land, thou, and all thy bands, and many people with thee. Thus saith the Lord God; It shall also come to pass, that at the same time shall things come into thy mind,*

and thou shalt think an evil thought: And thou shalt say, I will go up to the land of unwalled villages; I will go to them that are at rest, that dwell safely, all of them dwelling without walls, and having neither bars nor gates, To take a spoil, and to take a prey; to turn thine hand upon the desolate places that are now inhabited, and upon the people that are gathered out of the nations, which have gotten cattle and goods, that dwell in the midst of the land (in the center of the world).

Again, we see Antichrist as a source of war and death in Daniel 7:23, "*Thus he said, The fourth beast shall be the fourth kingdom upon earth, which shall be diverse from all kingdoms, and shall devour the whole earth, and shall tread it down, and break it in pieces.*"

MAHDI, A MAN OF WAR

War after war, Israel has defeated the Muslim hordes that have endeavored to wipe it off the face of the earth and drive it into the sea. According to Muslim tradition, the Mahdi will lead this army of black flags and will conquer Israel for Islam. The Muslims will slaughter Jews until few remain, and the Mahdi will set his headquarters in Jerusalem on the Temple Mount. Rasulullah (Mohammed) said: "Armies carrying black flags will come from Khurasan. No power will be able to stop them and they will finally reach Eela [Baitul Maqdas in Jerusalem] where they will erect their flags."[2] Note that Baitul Maqdas means "the holy house," referring to the Temple Mount in Jerusalem. The authors of the *Al-Mahdi and the End of Time* comment on the conquest as follows:

> The Mahdi will be victorious and eradicate those pigs and dogs and the idols of this time so there will once more be a caliphate based on prophethood as the Hadith states… Jerusalem will be the location of the rightly guided caliph-

ate and the center of Islamic rule, which will be headed by Imam al-Mahdi…That will abolish the leadership of the Jews…and put an end to the domination of Satans who spit evil into people and cause corruption in the earth, making them slaves of false idols and ruling the world by laws other than the Shari'a [Islamic law] of the Lord of the worlds.[3]

Another famous tradition tells of even the rocks and trees fighting against the Jews.

The Prophet said…the last hour would not come unless the Muslims will fight against the Jews and the Muslims would kill them until the Jews would hide themselves behind a stone or a tree and a stone or a tree would say: Muslim, or the servant of Allah, there is a Jew behind me; come and kill him.[4]

ALLAH'S STRANGE TITLE

Walid Shoebat points out that one of the ninety-nine names for Allah is *Al-Mumeet,* which means "the one who possesses the power of death, causer of death, the slayer, and the taker of life or the destroyer of life." The title is very similar to the title given to Satan in Revelation 9:11, *"And they had a king over them, which is the angel of the bottomless pit, whose name in the Hebrew tongue is Abaddon, but in the Greek tongue hath his name Apollyon."* The translation of Apollyon is destroyer.[5]

Who could motivate suicide bombers to walk into a crowded market place, detonate an attached bomb and blow dozens of innocent people into eternity? Who could put it into the minds of men to hijack commercial airplanes filled with innocent people and fly into skyscrapers killing thousands more? Who but *Al Mumeet*, the causer of death, the taker of life, the destroyer of life?

Contrast this with John 10:10, *"The thief cometh not, but for to steal, and to kill, and to destroy: I (Jesus) am come that they might have life, and that they might have it more abundantly."*

BOTH ANTICHRIST AND THE MAHDI HONOR GOD WITH THEIR GOLD AND SILVER

According to Daniel 11:38, the Antichrist honors the God of forces by accumulating riches from conquered peoples and lands. *"But in his estate shall he honour the God of forces: and a god whom his fathers knew not shall he honour with gold, and silver, and with precious stones, and pleasant things."* Muslims are obligated to give gifts called *zakat* ostensibly for helping the poor. Surah 9:60 teaches that the tax or gift involves more than just helping the poor.

> *Alms are only for the poor and the needy, and the officials (appointed) over them, and those whose hearts are made to incline (to truth) and the (ransoming of) captives and those in debts and in the **way of Allah** and the wayfarer; an ordinance from Allah; and Allah is knowing, Wise.*

The tax (zakat) is for the spread of Islam. Surah 9:34,35 makes this clear.

> *O you who believe! Most surely many of the doctors of law and the monks eat away the property of men falsely, and turn (them) from Allah's way; and (as for) those who hoard up gold and silver and do not spend it in **Allah's way**, announce to them a painful chastisement, On the day when it shall be heated in the fire of hell, then their foreheads and their sides and their backs shall be branded with it; this is what you hoarded up for yourselves, therefore taste what you hoarded.*

Of the more than 1,200 mosques in America, more than 80 per cent have been built with Saudi money. Saudi Arabia alone has spent $87 billion since 1973 to spread Islam throughout the United States and the western hemisphere.[6] Funding Muslim terrorist organizations by Muslim charities has resulted in the United States Homeland Security Administration's freezing dozens of Muslim zakat charities' accounts. The Mahdi, the perfecter of pure Islam, will certainly follow this practice of funding the spread of Islam through loot captured from their enemies.

BOTH ANTICHRIST AND THE MAHDI HONOR A GOD OF WAR AND ADVANCE HIS GLORY THROUGH WAR

Jihad is to Islam what evangelism is to Christianity. After His resurrection, five times. Christ gave His disciples the Great Commission. Acts 1:8 is one of the five. *"But ye shall receive power, after that the Holy Ghost is come upon you: and ye shall be witnesses unto me both in Jerusalem, and in all Judaea, and in Samaria, and unto the uttermost part of the earth."* After Pentecost and the filling of the Holy Spirit, in three hundred years, the disciples of Christ brought the Roman Empire to Christ. How did they do it? They did it with the **word**, i.e., the Word of God. They went out as sheep among wolves.

Six-hundred-twenty-two years later, a religious leader, Mohammed, came out of Arabia with a new revelation. "There is no god but Allah and Mohammed is his messenger." The program for disseminating Islam is called *jihad*, which literally means "struggle." After only one hundred years, the religion of Islam had spread out from Arabia to India in the east and to Spain in the west. How did they do it? They did it with the **sword**. The Muslims went out as wolves among sheep.

The punishment of those who wage war against Allah and

His apostle and strive to make mischief in the land is only this, that they should be murdered or crucified or **their hands and their feet should be cut off on opposite sides** *or they should be imprisoned; this shall be as a disgrace for them in this world, and in the hereafter they shall have a grievous chastisement.* (Surah 5:33)

To wage war against Allah is to reject the ultimatum, "There is no god but Allah and Mohammed is his messenger." Again, the Koran speaks as to how to treat the unbeliever. Surah 47:4,

So when you meet in battle those who disbelieve, then smite the necks (decapitate) until when you have overcome them, then make (them) prisoners, and afterwards either set them free as a favor or let them ransom (themselves) until the war terminates.

UNDERSTANDING JIHAD

Jihad is not going away, so we had best try to understand it. Walid Shoebat, at one time a jihadist in Palestine, gives a detailed definition:

Jihad is religious conditioning, using allusions of misery and glory days of the past in order to convert masses into becoming rage and pride-filled, remorseless killers and seekers of salvation by their own deaths. The goal is to re-establish a utopian theocratic world order where Allah and Muslims reign supreme and non-Muslims become subservient.[7]

That is what fundamental Islam is, and you will find out that everything in this dangerous movement fits within this definition. To cement in your mind just what jihad means to a Muslim, read a couple of quotes. Popular Muslim teacher Muhammad Saeed al-Qahtani says, "Jihad is an act of worship, it is one of the supreme forms of devotion to Allah. They say that jihad is only for defense. This lie must be exposed."[6] Again, Ibn Khaldun, a famous fourteenth century Islamic historian and philosopher, in his classic work, *The Muqaddimah*, defines jihad like this:

> In the Muslim community, the holy war is a religious duty, because of the universalism of the (Muslim) mission and (the obligation to) convert everybody to Islam either by **persuasion or by force**. Therefore, the caliphate (spiritual), the royal (government and military) authority is united in Islam, so the person in charge can devote the available strength to both of them at the same time.[9]

WHAT ABOUT THE CRUSADES?

Anyone who deals with Muslims will hear much of the Crusades. They cite the Crusades as justification for their jihad. The First Crusade was a military expedition by European Catholics to regain the Holy Lands taken by the Muslim conquest. It resulted in the capture of Jerusalem in 1099. It was launched in 1095 by Pope Urban II with the primary goal of repelling the invading Seljuk Turks from what is now Turkey. An additional goal soon became the principal objective: the Catholic reconquest of the sacred city of Jerusalem and the Holy Land, and the freeing of Christians from Islamic rule.[10]

The Crusades had no Biblical basis. They were carried out by the Roman Catholic Church and Pope Urban II, who promised indulgence for sins for those dying in the conflict. Pope Urban and those engaged in the Crusades ignored Jesus' words in Matthew 26:51,52,

And, behold, one of them which were with Jesus stretched out

his hand, and drew his sword, and struck a servant of the high priest's, and smote off his ear. Then said Jesus unto him, Put up again thy sword into his place: for all they that take the sword shall perish with the sword.

The Crusades were definitely an aberration from Christian teaching and principles. However, as we have seen, jihad is sometimes called the sixth pillar of Islam and is incumbent upon every true Muslim.

GOD OF FORCES

Daniel 11:38 is somewhat difficult to understand, so let us try to unravel it. *"But in his estate shall he honour the God of forces (*fortresses or war*): and a god whom his fathers knew not shall he honour with gold, and silver, and with precious stones, and pleasant things."* Think of all the religions of the world. The major ones are Christianity, Islam, Hinduism, Buddhism, Shintoism and Confucianism. Which one of these religions honors the God of forces? Which one of these religions uses force to convert people to its creed? Which one uses force to keep people in its fold? Of all the religions, only Islam honors the God of forces. So it is quite evident that the God of forces whom the Antichrist will honor is none but Mohammed's Allah. It is also quite evident that the Mahdi will honor the God of forces, Allah.

IS THE ANTICHRIST JEWISH?

How should we interpret *"a god whom his fathers knew not shall he honour with gold, and silver, and with precious stones, and pleasant things?"* "Fathers" does not refer to literal fathers or grandfathers, but rather to ancestors. In the event the Antichrist will be a Muslim, this could mean that he honors not the gods that were worshipped by the pagan Arabs of his ancestry. Rather, he worships and serves the God of forces, who is none other than Allah. The possibility of the Antichrist being non-Jewish is not strange. In fact, many teachers of prophecy reject the idea of a Jewish Antichrist. Speaking for many prophetic teachers, Arnold Fruchtenbaum, founder and director of Ariel Ministries, (a ministry to evangelize Jews) says,

> The fact that the plural form of the word 'god' (elohei) rather than Elohim is used makes this a reference to heathen deities and not to the God of Israel. There is much external evidence to show that this is the correct rendering of the Hebrew text.[11] Therefore, the Antichrist will not be a Jew but a Muslim.

CHAPTER SIX
THE MAHDI AND THE ANTICHRIST - CONTINUED

To recap our studies thus far we have seen the following similarities: both deny the Trinity, deny the Father and the Son, deny the deity of Christ, deny the cross, deny women's rights, claim to be the messiah, work false miracles, ride a white horse, are deceivers, attempt to change the times and laws, rule over ten entities, are the source of death and war, honor God with their gold and silver, honor a god of war and advance his glory through war. We will continue to see more similarities in this chapter as we compare the Antichrist and the Mahdi.

BOTH THE MAHDI AND THE ANTICHRIST CONDONE RAPE

Zechariah 14:2 attests to the fact that Antichrist and his soldiers will ravish (rape) the women of Jerusalem. *"For I will gather all nations against Jerusalem to battle; and the city shall be taken, and the houses rifled, and the women ravished; and half of the city shall go forth into captivity, and the residue of the people shall not be cut off from the city."* From the text it implies that looting houses and raping of women are part and parcel of their military tactics. The United States army will not tolerate its soldiers raping women. Any soldier found guilty will suffer dire consequences. Islam is the only religious system which legitimizes rape. Read the history of Islam and their battles and learn how they treated the women captives. Let one example suffice.

The Apostle of Allah sent a military expedition to Awtas at the battle of Hunain. They met their enemy and fought with them…Some of the Companions of the Apostle of Allah were reluctant to have intercourse with the female captives in the presence of their husbands who were unbelievers. Therefore, Allah the Exalted, sent down the Qur'anic verse "And all married women (are forbidden) unto you save those (captives) whom your right hand possess[es].[1]

Rape is common wherever Muslims live. The woman raped is usually blamed for inappropriate dress or misconduct which caused her to be raped. A Muslim woman who is raped brings great dishonor upon the family and suffers horribly. The rapist goes virtually unpunished.

Since the Mahdi will operate under Islamic principles it makes sense that looting and raping would characterize the way he would wage war.

BOTH THE MAHDI AND THE ANTICHRIST USHER IN A SEVEN YEAR PEACE TREATY

Daniel 9:27 speaks of Antichrist making a seven year covenant.

And he shall confirm the covenant with many for one week: and in the midst of the week he shall cause the sacrifice and the oblation to cease, and for the overspreading of abominations he shall make it desolate, even until the consummation, and that determined shall be poured upon the desolate (desolator).

Peace treaties between the Palestinians and Israel are nothing new. Most of us have heard of the Oslo Accord and other treaties initiated through the years. Notice that this covenant was confirmed rather than established. The "one week" speaks of seven years and in the "midst of the week" means three and a half years. After three and a half years Antichrist will break the covenant revealing his true identity and purpose. It is evident that at this time the Jewish Temple is once again present and the Jews are going through their ritual sacrifices. This could only happen if the Mahdi had given them permission to do so. The Antichrist will cause the temple worship to cease and will desecrate the Holy of Holies. He will declare war on Israel and institute his "final solution" i.e., the extermination of all Jews. This was all foretold by Jesus in Matthew 24:15-25.

> *When ye therefore shall see the abomination of desolation, spoken of by Daniel the prophet, stand in the holy place, (whoso readeth, let him understand:) Then let them which be in Judaea flee into the mountains: Let him which is on the housetop not come down to take any thing out of his house: Neither let him which is in the field return back to take his clothes. And woe unto them that are with child, and to them that give suck in those days! But pray ye that your flight be not in the winter, neither on the sabbath day: For then shall be great tribulation, such as was not since the beginning of the world to this time, no, nor ever shall be. And except those days should be shortened, there should no flesh be saved: but for the elect's sake those days shall be shortened. Then if any man shall say unto you, Lo, here is Christ, or there; believe it not. For there shall arise false Christs, and false prophets, and shall shew great signs and wonders; insomuch that, if it were possible, they shall deceive the very elect. Behold, I have told you before.*

It seems stranger than fiction that Islamic tradition records the same event as our Bible. Read these words from the Hadith.

> Hadhrat Abu Umamah says that Rasulullah (Mohammed) said: "There will be four peace agreements between you and the Romans. The fourth agreement will be mediated through a person who will be from the progeny of Hadhrat Haroon (Aaron) and will be upheld for seven years."[2]

This quote signifies that the Mahdi will make four covenants with the Romans. Joel Richardson, in his book the Islamic Antichrist, makes this comment:

> While there is more than one tradition regarding the nature and timing of the Mahdi's ascendancy to power, one particular hadith places the events at the final peace agreement between the Arabs and the Romans (Romans refer to Christians or more generally the West). Although the peace agreement is made with the Romans, it is presumably mediated through a Jew from the priestly lineage of Aaron. The peace agreement will be made for seven years.[3]

BOTH THE MAHDI AND THE ANTICHRIST DECEIVE AND DESTROY BY PEACE

The lie that "Islam is a religion of peace" has been told so often by so many that to dispute this outrageous falsehood brands one as an "Islamophobe." A cursory study of the history of Islam reveals from its inception to the present that violence, force, and intimidation characterize Islam. One of the most revered Muslim leaders of all time, the late Ayatollah Khomeini said, "The purest joy in Islam is to kill and to be killed." Even Mr. No Spin himself, Bill O'Reilly, recently took Pat Roberson to the woodshed for telling the truth about Islam. Without exaggeration it can be said that every week somewhere in the world Muslims kill Christians, burn homes and churches. Yet the media looks the other way. Why is this? Political correctness rules the roost. People in public life who dare to buck the trend by telling the truth pay a dear price. Michelle Malkin, conservative columnist, explains political correctness and its danger.

> Political correctness is a gangrenous infection. My gen-

eration has submitted to a toxic diet of multiculturalism, identity politics, anti-Americanism, and entitlement. The problem festered under the Bush administration. Despite 9/11, government at all levels refused to screen out jihadi-apologizing influences in our military, at the FBI, in prisons and even fire departments. Despite the bloody consequences of open borders, the Bush Pentagon allowed illegal aliens to enter the military. The grievance lobby has plied the Muslim jihadist-as-victim narrative for nearly a decade now.[4]

Daniel 8:25 says that Antichrist ". . . *and by peace shall destroy many* . . ." In the context of Antichrist's seven year covenant (peace treaty) with Israel and the West, the purpose was to disarm, deceive and ultimately destroy his enemies by peace. Any student of Islam will be aware of hudna an Arabic term for a peace treaty which purpose is to buy time by producing a truce in order to equip and prepare for another attack. Shira A. Drissman, an Israeli spokesman said,

What is being touted as a 'cease-fire' is something called a 'hudna.' A hudna [also known as a hudibiyya or khudaibiya] is a tactical cease-fire that allows the Arabs to rebuild their terrorist infrastructure in order to be more effective when the "cease-fire" is called off." [5]

This practice of treaty making for ulterior motives evidences great similarity between the Biblical Antichrist and the Muslim Mahdi.

BOTH THE MAHDI AND THE ANTICHRIST DESIRE WORLD DOMINATION

The Bible pictures Antichrist as pursuing world conquest by

both peace treaties and actual warfare. Revelation 13:7 tells us about his making war and his power over all nations. *"And it was given unto him to make war with the saints, and to overcome them: and power was given him over all kindreds, and tongues, and nations."* Our country and the liberal media refuse to acknowledge Islam's program for world domination. When speaking to American audiences Muslim leaders deny or downplay jihad i.e., subjugating the world to Islam. When speaking to their own, the message of jihad is crystal clear. A quote from Muslim scholar Mawlana Sayid Abul Ala Mawdudi very clearly states Islam's plan to dominate the world.

> Islam is not a normal religion like other religions in the world, and Muslim nations are not like normal nations. Muslim nations are very special because they have a command from Allah to rule the entire world and to be over every nation in the world. Islam is a revolutionary faith that comes to destroy any government made by man. Islam doesn't look for a nation to be in a better condition than another nation. Islam doesn't care about the land or who owns the land. The goal of Islam is to rule the entire world and submit all of mankind to the faith of Islam. Any nation or power that gets in the way of that goal, Islam will fight and destroy it. In order to fulfill that goal, Islam can use every power available every way it can be used to bring worldwide revolution. This is jihad.[6]

BOTH THE MAHDI AND THE ANTICHRIST LEAD A TURKISH-IRANIAN INVASION

Zechariah 9:13, *"When I have bent Judah for me, filled the bow with Ephraim, and raised up thy sons, O Zion, against thy sons, O Greece, and made thee as the sword of a mighty man"* speaks of a battle between Israel and Javan. Javan or Ionia is sometimes translated

"Greece" but is a province located on the west coast of modern Turkey.[7] This battle is alluded to in Ezekiel 38 and a coalition of forces from Turkey, Persia, modern day Iran, and other surrounding countries will march on Israel. In the Biblical account God intercedes for Israel and destroys the invading forces. Muslim traditions predict that these same countries will march against Israel. Abdul Rahman al-Wahabi in the Day of Wrath writes of this battle.

> The final battle will be waged by the Muslim faithful coming on the back of horses…carrying black flags. They will stand on the east side of the Jordan River and will wage war that the earth has never seen before. The true Messiah who is the Islamic Mahdi will defeat Europe, will lead this army of Seljuks [Turks]. He will preside over the world from Jerusalem because Mecca would have been destroyed.[8]

Turkey for many years has been the only secular Muslim nation. Until recently they have sided with the West and Israel. Things are changing. World Magazine reports in its November 21, 2009 issue an article Switching Sides.

> A major shift has taken place in the geopolitics of the Middle East. Turkey, a strategic ally of the West and Israel - and the only Muslim country with a secular government besides fractured Iraq- has effectively signaled that it's leaving its Western friends and reorienting itself eastward… The transformation suggests more than a new political calculus. Caroline Glick, editor of The Jerusalem Post, says, 'Part of the reason for Turkey's embrace of Syria is that the Turks have been carefully advancing the notion that Turkey may emerge as a neo-Ottoman caliphate.'[9]

Turkey will be a big time player in the years that lie ahead. These developments reinforce the fact that armies will indeed come from Turkey and surrounding areas to attack Israel.

BOTH THE MAHDI AND THE ANTICHRIST PRACTICE BEHEADING

Revelation 20:4, has caught my attention for several years.

And I saw thrones, and they sat upon them, and judgment was given unto them: and I saw the souls of them that were beheaded for the witness of Jesus, and for the word of God, and which had not worshipped the beast, neither his image, neither had received his mark upon their foreheads, or in their hands; and they lived and reigned with Christ a thousand years.

The Antichrist will behead those who refuse to take the mark of the beast. Beheading is not a common method of execution in the world today.

The guillotine was a device used for carrying out executions by decapitation. It consists of a tall upright frame from which a blade is suspended. This blade is raised with a rope and then allowed to drop, severing the head from the body. The device is noted for long being the main method of execution in France and, more particularly, for its use during the French Revolution, when it "became a part of popular culture, celebrated as the people's avenger by supporters of the Revolution and vilified as the pre-eminent symbol of the Terror by opponents". Nevertheless, the guillotine continued to be used long after the French Revolution in several countries.[10]

Beheading as a method of execution is not peculiar to Islam. It has been practiced in China, Japan, England and many other countries. But in recent years beheading and the death penalty itself has been banned in most countries. The Koran commands Muslims to "strike the necks" of their enemies. Only a historical revisionist or a lying Islamophile would deny that Muslims are infamous for using the sword to decapitate. The historical evidence is overwhelming.

NICK BERG'S AND DANIEL PEARL'S DECAPITATION

Nicholas Evan Berg was an American Jewish businessman who went to Iraq after the US invasion of Iraq. He was abducted and later beheaded according to a video released in May 2004 by individuals claiming to be Islamic militants. The CIA claimed that Abu Musab al-Zarqawi personally beheaded Berg. The decapitation was released on the Internet, reportedly from London to a Malaysian hosted homepage by the Islamic organization al-Ansars. His killers claimed that his death was carried out to avenge abuses of Iraqi prisoners by U.S. soldiers at Abu Ghraib prison.[11]

Daniel Pearl was an American journalist captured by Muslim militants while serving in Pakistan. A video shows what happened. The actual beheading is thankfully not shown, but we do see the severed head afterward. What really happens in this video is this: Pearl gives a little pre-prepared speech listing some of the demands of his captors. Pearl also makes some impromptu remarks about his Jewish ethnicity, that of his family, his family's Jewish religion, the fact that his family are Zionists, and a town in Israel that is named after his great-grandfather, a famous Zionist. While Pearl is making all these remarks about Israel, Zionism, Judaism, etc., there are interspersed photos of Israeli troops hassling and arresting Palestinians, of dead Palestinians, etc. Then it shows Pearl on the ground, already dead, thank God, apparently with his throat slit, while an unknown man, possibly KSM, easily saws off the head and then holds it up. The severed head stays up for the rest of the video while the group names itself – the National Movement for Pakistan Sovereignty, and lists a number of nationalist demands – the return of all Pakistani prisoners from Guantanamo, the release of all prisoners from Guantanamo, the release of F-16's that Pakistan bought from the US and never received, and an end to all US presence in

Pakistan. Then it says, "We assure Americans that they will never be safe on the Muslim land of Pakistan." This is followed by, "And if our demands are not met, this scene shall be repeated again and again and again..."[12]

MUSLIMS DENIAL OF BEHEADING

Imam Muhammad Adam al-Sheikh, head of the Dar al-Hijrah mosque in Falls Church, Virginia, for example, claimed incorrectly that "beheadings are not mentioned in the Koran at all." Asma Afsaruddin, an associate professor of Arabic and Islamic studies at the University of Notre Dame, also misrepresented Islamic theology and history when she told a reporter, "There is absolutely no religious imperative for this. (beheading)" The Council on American-Islamic Relations (CAIR) as well as the American Anti-Arab Discrimination Committee (ADC) have both signed on to a statement that such killings "did not represent the tenets of Islam." Sam Hamod, former director of the Islamic Center in Washington, D.C., claimed that the Qur'anic passages on beheading unbelievers did not actually mean that people should be killed. Such fulminations (denunciations) have had an effect: the Western news media has, perhaps as a result of political correctness or its own bias, twisted the reality of Islamic history and propagated such revisionism. With such apologetics, Western academics either display basic ignorance of their fields or purposely mislead. The intelligentsia's denial of any religious roots to the recent spate of decapitation has parallels in the logical back flips and kid-glove treatments in which many professors engaged in order to deny a religious basis for violent jihad. Afsaruddin and Hamod aside, Islamists justify murder and decapitation with both theological citations and historical precedent.[13]

DECAPITATION IN ISLAMIC THEOLOGY

Tradition justifies the decapitation of prisoners with Qur'anic scripture. Surah (chapter) 47 contains the ayah (verse): *"When you encounter the unbelievers on the battlefield, strike off their heads until you have crushed them completely; then bind the prisoners tightly."* With little variation, scholars have translated the verse as, *"When you meet the unbelievers, smite their necks."* Another, albeit less-frequently, cited Qur'anic passage also sanctions beheadings of non-Muslims. Surah 8:12 reads: *"I will cast dread into the hearts of the unbelievers. Strike off their heads, then, and strike off all of their fingertips."* The point of this opening phrase—to "cast dread" or, as some translations have it, "instill terror"—has now been adopted by Islamist terrorists to justify decapitation of hostages.[14]

While some Islamists might justify murder of prisoners on Qur'anic prescription, others reinforce their conclusions by drawing analogies to events during the almost 1,400 years of Islamic history. Here beheading of captives is a recurring theme. Both Islamic regimes and their opposition have utilized beheadings as both military and judicial policy. The practice of beheading non-Muslim captives extends back to the Prophet himself. Ibn Ishaq (d. 768 C.E.), the earliest biographer of Muhammad, is recorded as saying that the Prophet ordered the execution by decapitation of 700 men of the Jewish Banu Qurayza tribe in Medina for allegedly plotting against him. Islamic leaders from Muhammad's time until today have followed his model. Examples of decapitation, of both the living and the dead, in Islamic history are myriad. Yusuf b. Tashfin (d. 1106) led the Al-Murabit (Almoravid) Empire to conquer from western Sahara to central Spain. After the battle of Zallaqa in 1086, he had 24,000 corpses of the defeated Castilians beheaded "and piled them up to make a sort of minaret for the muezzins who, standing on the piles of headless cadavers, sang the praises of Allah." He then had the detached heads sent to all the major cities of North Africa and Spain as an example of Christian impotence. The

Al-Murabits were conquered the following century by the Al-Muwahhids (Almohads), under whose rule Castilian Christian enemies were beheaded after any lost battles.

The Ottoman Empire was the decapitation state par excellence. Upon the Ottoman victory over Christian Serbs at the battle of Kosovo in 1389, the Muslim army beheaded the Serbian king and scores of Christian prisoners. At the battle of Varna in 1444, the Ottomans beheaded King Ladislaus of Hungary and "put his head at the tip of a long pike … and brandished it toward the Poles and Hungarians." Upon the fall of Constantinople, the Ottomans sent the head of the dead Byzantine emperor on tour to major cities in the sultan's domains. The Ottomans even beheaded at least one Eastern Orthodox patriarch. In 1456, the sultan allowed the grand mufti of the empire to personally decapitate King Stephen of Bosnia and his sons—even though they had surrendered and, seven decades later, the sultan ordered 2,000 Hungarian prisoners beheaded. In the early nineteenth century, even the British fell victim to the Ottoman scimitar. An 1807 British expedition to Egypt resulted in "a few hundred spiked British heads left rotting in the sun outside Rosetta."[15]   Evidence keeps building that the Antichrist of the Bible and the Mahdi of Islam have so many similarities that it is beyond the pale of happenstance. In the next chapter we will bring to your attention a few more similarities.

CHAPTER SEVEN
THE MAHDI AND THE ANTICHRIST - CONTINED

In this chapter we will complete the task of comparing the Antichrist of the Bible with the Mahdi of Muslim traditions, the Hadith. To refresh our memories thus far we have seen the following similarities: both deny the Trinity, deny the Father and the Son, deny the deity of Christ, deny the cross, deny women's rights, claim to be the messiah, work false miracles, ride a white horse, are deceivers, attempt to change the times and laws, rule over ten entities, are the source of death and war, honor God with their gold and silver, honor a god of war and advance his glory through war, condone rape, usher in a seven year peace treaty, deceive and destroy by peace, desire world domination, lead a Turkish-Iranian invasion of Israel, and practice beheading. There are still some striking similarities to be noted.

BOTH THE MAHDI AND THE ANTICHRIST DESIRE ISRAEL'S DESTRUCTION

Muslims have a diabolical hatred of Jews and Israel. As Mohammed began his ministry, he courted the Jews and Christians. He even commanded his followers to pray toward Jerusalem. In the early surahs or chapters of the Koran, he dealt gently with Jews and Christians, calling them the people of the book. Surah 2:62:

> *Surely those who believe, and those who are Jews, and the Christians, and the Sabians, whoever believes in Allah and the Last day and does good, they shall have their reward from*

their Lord, and there is no fear for them, nor shall they grieve.

He was doing this to woo them to follow him and his new religion. Both Jews and Christians were loyal to their book and were somewhat amused at Mohammed's misunderstanding of Biblical history. Once they turned their backs on Mohammed and his new religion of Islam, his attitude and message toward Christians and Jews abruptly changed. Surah 2:64-66,

> *Then you turned back after that; so were it not for the grace of Allah and His mercy on you, you would certainly have been among the losers. And certainly you have known those among you who exceeded the limits of the Sabbath, so We said to them: Be (as) apes, despised and hated. So We made them an example to those who witnessed it and those who came after it, and an admonition to those who guard (against evil).*

Allah, in giving Mohammed the Koran, changed his mind so many times that a policy had to be devised to give a cover. Muslims developed *Nasekh,* a hermeneutical rule that overrides the tolerant and peaceful verses that Islam considers obsolete or *Mansookh* and replace them with orders to fight and kill the unbelievers (infidels*).* Surah 9:29,

> *Fight those who do not believe in Allah, nor in the latter day, nor do they prohibit what Allah and His Apostle have prohibited, nor follow the religion of truth, out of those who have been given the Book, until they pay the tax in acknowledgment of superiority and they are in a state of subjection.*

Koranic revelation is progressive and the newer verses cancel out the older verses.

ANTICHRIST'S FINAL SOLUTION

Long before Islam's arrival, the Bible speaks of Antichrist's plan to destroy the Jews. Revelation 12:2-5 describes Antichrist's attempt to destroy the infant Jesus and his failure to do so.

And she being with child cried, travailing in birth, and pained to be delivered. And there appeared another wonder in heaven; and behold a great red dragon, having seven heads and ten horns, and seven crowns upon his heads.. and the dragon stood before the woman which was ready to be delivered, for to devour her child as soon as it was born. And she brought forth a man child, who was to rule all nations with a rod of iron: and her child was caught up unto God, and to his throne.

Verses 13-16 give us more details of Israel's deliverance.

And when the dragon saw that he was cast unto the earth, he persecuted the woman which brought forth the man child. And to the woman were given two wings of a great eagle, that she might fly into the wilderness, into her place, where she is nourished for a time, and times, and half a time, from the face of the serpent. And the serpent cast out of his mouth water as a flood after the woman, that he might cause her to be carried away of the flood. And the earth helped the woman, and the earth opened her mouth, and swallowed up the flood which the dragon cast out of his mouth.

The mention of time, times, and half a time date this event. It is during the Great Tribulation, the last three and one-half years of Antichrist's reign. This providential rescue saves Israel from extinction.

Revelation 13:5-7 sums up Antichrist's rage against God and

His people.

> *And there was given unto him a mouth speaking great things and blasphemies; and power was given unto him to continue forty and two months. And he opened his mouth in blasphemy against God, to blaspheme his name, and his tabernacle, and them that dwell in heaven. And it was given unto him to make war with the saints, and to overcome them: and power was given him over all kindreds, and tongues, and nations.*

HITLER LOVED ISLAM

As an aside, let us look at what Hitler thought of Islam. Walid Shoebat, quotes Albert Speer's memoirs:

> On an occasion Hitler expounded his views on Christianity to a visiting delegation of Arabs. Discussing the implication of the battle of Tours, when Charles Martel, a German, defeated the advancing Muslim army, Hitler held forth, "Had the Arabs won the battle, the world would be Mohammedan today. For theirs was a religion that believed in spreading the faith by the sword and subjugating all nations to that faith. The Germanic people would have become heirs to that religion. Such a creed was perfectly suited for the German temperament.[1]

Hitler said that the conquering Arabs, because of their racial inferiority, would in the long run have been unable to contend with the harsher climate and conditions of the country. They could not have kept down the more vigorous natives, so that ultimately, not Arabs but Islamized Germans could have stood at the head of the Mohammedan Empire.[2] Hitler summed it up like this:

You see it is our misfortune to have the wrong religion. Why didn't we have the religion of the Japanese, who regard sacrifice for the Fatherland as the highest good? The Mohammedan religion too would have been much more compatible than Christianity. Why did it have to be Christianity with its meekness and flabbiness?[3]

Hitler learned some lessons from Islam. In the early 1900's the Ottoman Turks conducted a holocaust against Christians in Turkey and Armenia. The Turks developed methods such as putting 90 people in box cars with a capacity of 36 and leaving them there for days.

Hitler was even more impressed that the Turks got away with genocide. On August 22, 1939, Hitler explained his plans to invade Poland including the formation of death squads that would exterminate men, women, and children. He asked, "Who, after all, speaks today of the annihilation of the Armenians?"[4]

Heinrich Himmler also had a good opinion of Islam. Heinrich Himmler, a high ranking Nazi stated, "I have nothing against Islam because it educates the men in this division for me and promises heaven if they fight and are killed in action, a very practical and attractive religion for soldiers.[5]

ANTISEMITISM IN ISLAM

The Koran spews forth venom and hatred against the Jews. The hatred is so intense that not one single Jew is allowed to reside in Saudi Arabia. The Koran says in Surah 5:59, 60,

Say: O followers of the Book! do you find fault with us (for aught) except that we believe in Allah and in what has been revealed to us and what was revealed before, and that most of you are transgressors?

> *Say: Shall I inform you of (him who is) worse than this in retribution from Allah? (Worse is he) whom Allah has cursed and brought His wrath upon, and of whom He made apes and swine, and he who served the Shaitan; these are worse in place and more erring from the straight path.*

Not only the Koran, but the Hadith also belches out hate against the Jews. This famous quotation is quoted in Mosques worldwide:

> The last hour would not come unless the Muslims fight against the Jews and the Muslims would kill them until the Jews would hide themselves behind a stone or a tree and a stone or a tree would say: 'Oh, faithful Muslim, or the servant of Allah, there is a Jew behind me; come and kill him.[6]

The hadith goes on to say more about the Mahdi's hatred of the Jews: "The Mahdi will slaughter the Jews and the women who are following the Dajjal (Christ)."[7]

We have noted before that Muslims believe Jesus is coming to earth again. In Islam, one of the main reasons for his coming is to refute the controversy that they killed Jesus. The Muslim Jesus fights against the Jews at the Gate of Hudd and kills the Dajjal. He will have 70,000 Jewish followers. The final war between the Jews and the Muslims will ensue, and the Muslims will be victorious.[8]

BOTH THE MAHDI AND THE ANTICHRIST OCCUPY THE TEMPLE MOUNT

Why do both the Antichrist and the Mahdi desire to occupy the Temple Mount? The temple in Jerusalem with its Holy of Holies was the dwelling place of God. As for the Antichrist, he wants to be worshipped as God. Paul makes this clear in 2 Thessalonians

2:3,4,

> *Let no man deceive you by any means: for that day shall not come, except there come a falling away first, and that man of sin be revealed, the son of perdition; Who opposeth and exalteth himself above all that is called God, or that is worshipped; so that he as God sitteth in the temple of God, shewing himself that he is God.*

The Mahdi's desire to occupy the Temple Mount is not hard to figure out. Jerusalem has been a "cup of trembling" (Zechariah 12:2) and a "burdensome stone" (Zechariah 12:3) throughout history. Mohammed's companions captured Jerusalem shortly after his death. Then the Crusaders recaptured it and eventually lost it. Jerusalem, by the way, is the geographical center of planet earth; battles have been waged over her for centuries. Islam's supreme desire is to kill the Jews and take over Jerusalem and make it the headquarters for their Caliphate (Muslim government). So far all the Islamic countries combined have not been able to defeat the Jews and reclaim Jerusalem for their own.

Egyptian authors, Muhammad ibn Izzat and Muhammad 'Arif comment on the tradition of the army of the black flags (Mahdi's army) marching on Jerusalem:

> The Mahdi will be victorious and eradicate those pigs and dogs and idols of this time so that there will once more be a caliphate based on prophethood as the Hadith states… Jerusalem will be the location of the rightly guided caliphate and the center of Islamic rule, which will be headed by Imam al-Mahdi…That will abolish the leadership of the Jews…and put an end to the domination of the Satans who spit evil into people and cause corruption in the earth, making them slaves of false idols, and ruling by laws other than Sharia (Islamic Law) of the Lords of the world.[9]

BOTH THE MAHDI AND THE ANTICHRIST ENJOY DESECRATING BODIES

It will be an interesting time when the two witnesses will harass the Antichrist. How frustrated he will be that no weapons formed against them would work. Revelation 11:7-12 describes the ministry, death, desecration and resurrection of the two witnesses.

And when they shall have finished their testimony, the beast that ascendeth out of the bottomless pit shall make war against them, and shall overcome them, and kill them. And their dead bodies shall lie in the street of the great city, which spiritually is called Sodom and Egypt, where also our Lord was crucified. And they of the people and kindreds and tongues and nations shall see their dead bodies three days and an half, and shall not suffer their dead bodies to be put in graves. And they that dwell upon the earth shall rejoice over them, and make merry, and shall send gifts one to another; because these two prophets tormented them that dwelt on the earth. And after three days and an half the Spirit of life from God entered into them, and they stood upon their feet; and great fear fell upon them which saw them. And they heard a great voice from heaven saying unto them, Come up hither. And they ascended up to heaven in a cloud; and their enemies beheld them.

Talk about drama!

The Antichrist and his government's refusal to give proper burial to these two witnesses illustrate this point. Instead they put the bodies on public display and celebrate the occasion with festivity. The Bible does not tell us who these two witnesses will be, but I would like to take a guess. As far I know, the only two men in the Bible who went to heaven without dying were Enoch and Elijah. So I vote that the two witnesses were these two because the Bible says,

Hebrews 9:27, *"As it is appointed unto men once to die, but after this the judgment."*

ISLAM'S HISTORY OF DESECRATING BODIES

Most of us remember Mogadishu, Somalia, in 1993, when the naked body of the dead American soldier was dragged through the streets while the people wildly cheered. In Iraq, the charred bodies of American engineers were strung up for all to see and thus celebrate the death of the infidels. Can any of us forget watching the Palestinians dancing in the streets celebrating the destruction of the twin towers and the deaths of 1,400 infidels? In February of 2007, in Saudi Arabia, America's biggest Arab ally, four men charged with robbery were publicly beheaded and crucified. *The al-Ridadh Newspaper* gave the following account:

> The bodies of four Sri Lankans beheaded in Saudi Arabia have gone on public display, in what was said to be an effort to halt a rise in crime committed by foreigners. After the men were crucified, their bodies were tied to wooden beams after beheading—as part of moves to deter other foreigners from crime…The desert kingdom, home to Islam's holiest shrines, says it applies strict Islamic law.[10]

Since the Mahdi will be a strict Muslim under Islamic law, we can expect the same of him.

ISLAM'S ANTICHRIST OUR MESSIAH; ISLAM'S MESSIAH OUR ANTICHRIST

In the eyes of the Muslims, our returning Lord is a wicked, ugly, heinous individual known as Al Dajjal in Muslim tradition.

The Dajjal will fight on the side of the Jews. He is said to be a great deceiver with miraculous powers. Kabbani in his book, *The Approach of Armageddon? An Islamic Perspective,* gives an interesting description.

> The Prophet was warning us that in the Last Days there would be someone who would deceive all humanity. The Dajjal will possess power over this world. Thus, Muslims must be careful not to have the love of the world in their hearts so they won't leave their religion and follow him. He will be able to heal the sick by wiping his hand on them, like Jesus did, but with deceit the Dajjal will lead people down the path to hell. Thus the Dajjal is the false Messiah, or Antichrist (Massih ad-Dajjal). He will pretend to be the messiah, and deceive people by showing amazing powers.[11]

Muslims scholars believe that the Dajjal will claim to be Jesus Christ and will claim to be God. The Jews, of course, reject Jesus Christ as their messiah, but they look for a messiah to come and save them and set up the kingdom of David. Concerning the Jewish hope of a messiah, Imam Sheikh Ibrahim Mahdi of the Palestinian Authority, had this to say:

> The Jews await the false Messiah, while we await with Allah's help…the Mahdi and Jesus, peace be upon him. Jesus' pure hands will murder the false Jewish messiah. Where? In the city of Lod, in Palestine. Palestine will be, as it was in the past, a graveyard for the invaders.[12]

THE JEWISH MESSIAH IS THE LORD CHRIST

Zechariah 12:10,11 speaks of the Lord returning to save His people and the city of Jerusalem from the forces of the Antichrist.

> *And I will pour upon the house of David, and upon the inhabitants of Jerusalem, the spirit of grace and of supplications: and they shall look upon me whom they have pierced, and they shall mourn for him, as one mourneth for his only son, and shall be in bitterness for him, as one that is in bitterness for his firstborn. In that day shall there be a great mourning in Jerusalem, as the mourning of Hadadrimmon in the valley of Megiddon.*

The Antichrist, i.e., the Mahdi, will lead his army in pillaging the city and raping the women. When all hope is lost, the Jews will see Christ, whom they pierced, and will repent of their unbelief and rejection of their Messiah. They will follow their resurrected Lord to victory. Seeing the Jews following Christ, the Muslims will believe that this one is indeed the Dajjal they have been taught to fear. They gather themselves to their Mahdi and his army with the black flags. Revelation 19:19-21 tells us the end of the story.

> *And I saw the beast, and the kings of the earth, and their armies, gathered together to make war against him that sat on the horse, and against his army. And the beast was taken, and with him the false prophet that wrought miracles before him, with which he deceived them that had received the mark of the beast, and them that worshipped his image. These both were cast alive into a lake of fire burning with brimstone. And the remnant were slain with the sword of him that sat upon the horse, which sword proceeded out of his mouth: and all the fowls were filled with their flesh.*

I am deeply grateful to Walid Shoebat and Joel Richardson for bringing these evident truths to my attention. As we conclude our study comparing the Biblical Antichrist with the Muslim Mahdi, the similarities are astonishing: both the Antichrist and the Mahdi deny the Trinity, the Father and the Son, the deity of Christ, the cross, and women's rights. Both the Antichrist and the Mahdi claim to be the messiah, work false miracles, ride a white horse, attempt to change the times and laws, rule over ten entities, honor their god with their gold and silver, honor a god of war, condone rape, usher in a seven year peace treaty, deceive and destroy by peace, desire world domination, and lead a Turkish-Iranian invasion of Israel. They also practice beheading, hate Israel, occupy the Temple Mount, and enjoy desecrating dead bodies. The Muslims' Mahdi is the Christians' Antichrist, and the Christians' returning Lord Jesus Christ is the Muslims' Dajjal. All these similarities convince me that the Muslim Mahdi will indeed be the Antichrist of the Bible.

CHAPTER EIGHT
JESUS IN THE KORAN, THE HADITH, AND THE BIBLE

Undoubtedly Jesus Christ of Nazareth presents the world's religions, especially Islam, with a claim that is difficult for them to accept: *"Jesus said, I am the way, the truth, and the life: no man cometh unto the Father, but by me"* (John 14:6). Six hundred years later a man in Arabia claimed that the angel of Allah, Jibriel (Gabriel), revealed to him, *"There is no god but Allah, and Mohammed is his messenger."* The purpose of this chapter is to learn how Islam has dealt with Jesus and His claim.

WHAT THE KORAN SAYS ABOUT JESUS

The Koran makes eleven statements about Jesus. Various surahs (chapters) speak to the subject: dealing with the miraculous conception of Jesus, Surah 66:12 says, *"And Marium, the daughter of Imran, who guarded her chastity, so We breathed into her of Our inspiration and she accepted the truth of the words of her Lord and His books, and she was of, the obedient ones."*

Surah 19:19-21 speaks of Jesus' miraculous birth.

He said: I am only a messenger of your Lord: That I will give you a pure boy. She said: When shall I have a boy and no mortal has yet touched me, nor have I been unchaste? He said: Even so; your Lord says: It is easy to Me: and that We may make him a sign to men and a mercy from Us, and it is a matter which has been decreed.

Surah 19:27-33 tells us that Jesus was born with the ability of speech, i.e., He spoke at His birth.

> *And she came to her people with him, carrying him (with her). They said: O Marium! Surely you have done a strange thing. O sister of Haroun! Your father was not a bad man, nor, was your mother an unchaste woman. But she pointed to him. They said: How should we speak to one who was a child in the cradle? He said: Surely I am a servant of Allah; He has given me the Book and made me a prophet; And He has made me blessed wherever I may be, and He has enjoined on me prayer and poor-rate so long as I live; And dutiful to my mother, and He has not made me insolent, unblessed; And peace on me on the day I was born, and on the day I die, and on the day I am raised to life.*

Jesus was not like other men, as He had supernatural knowledge. Surah 3:48, says, *"And He will teach him (Jesus) the Book and the wisdom and the Tavrat and the Injeel."*

Surah 19:31 says in some special way Jesus was blessed. *"And He has made me blessed wherever I may be, and He has enjoined on me prayer and poor-rate so long as I live."*

Jesus is endowed with the Holy Spirit. Surah 2:87 says, *"And most certainly We gave Musa the Book and We sent apostles after him one after another; and We gave Isa, the son of Marium, clear arguments and strengthened him with the holy spirit."*

Jesus is the Word of God. Surah 4:171 says,

> *O followers of the Book! do not exceed the limits in your religion, and do not speak (lies) against Allah, but (speak) the truth; the Messiah, Isa son of Marium is only an apostle of Allah and His Word which He communicated to Marium and a spirit from Him.*

Jesus is Allah's Messiah. Surah 39:44, 45 says,

> *When the angels said: O Marium, surely Allah gives you good news with a Word from Him (of one) whose name is the Messiah, Isa son of Marium, worthy of regard in this world and the hereafter and of those who are made near (to Allah).*

Jesus has the power to create, heal and raise the dead. Surah 5:110, 3:49 says,

> *When Allah will say: O Isa son of Marium! Remember My favor on you and on your mother, when I strengthened you I with the holy Spirit, you spoke to the people in the cradle and I when of old age, and when I taught you the Book and the wisdom and the Taurat and the Injeel; and when you determined out of clay a thing like the form of a bird by My permission, then you breathed into it and it became a bird by My permission, and you healed the blind and the leprous by My permission; and when you brought forth the dead by My permission; and when I withheld the children of Israel from you when you came to them with clear arguments, but those who disbelieved among them said: This is nothing but clear enchantment.*

The Koran has negative comments on Jesus' death and resurrection. Surah 4:157-158 says,

> *And their saying: Surely we have killed the Messiah, Isa son of Marium, the apostle of Allah; and they did not kill him nor did they crucify him, but it appeared to them so (like Isa) and most surely those who differ therein are only in a doubt about it; they have no knowledge respecting it, but only follow a conjecture, and they killed him not for sure. Nay! Allah took him up to Himself; and Allah is Mighty and wise.*

Jesus ascended and will return. Surah 3:55 says,

And when Allah said: O Isa, I am going to terminate the period of your stay (on earth) and cause you to ascend unto Me and purify you of those who disbelieve and make those who follow you above those who disbelieve to the day of resurrection; then to Me shall be your return, so l will decide between you concerning that in which you differed.

The Koran gives Jesus a back-handed compliment. It tells us that He had a miraculous birth; was the Messiah of Allah, the Word of God, endowed with the Holy Spirit, and a man with powers to create, heal, raise the dead; had supernatural knowledge and is blessed. Yet the Koran denies the three most important aspects of Jesus' life: His incarnation, His death on the cross and His resurrection from the dead. To believe that Jesus is the Almighty God (Revelation 1:8, *"I am Alpha and Omega, the beginning and the ending, saith the Lord, which is, and which was, and which is to come, the Almighty."*) is to commit *shirk*, the unpardonable sin. The Koran criminalizes those who believe that Jesus is who He said He was.

As we have pointed out before, Muslims believe that Jesus did not die on the cross. Allah made the person who was crucified look like Jesus. Allah caused the real Jesus to ascend to heaven without dying. Now the plot thickens. Jesus does indeed return to earth, but not as Christians expect. While in heaven He has become a radical Muslim. His purpose for returning is to force Jews and Tribulation believers to turn to Islam on threat of death if they refuse. Jesus also has the honor of killing Dajjal, Islam's Antichrist, who is our Lord, coming in glory to rule and reign.

WHAT THE HADITH SAYS ABOUT JESUS

The Hadith, the Muslim tradition, uses several names for Jesus. The most common name is Isa. Sometimes He is called Hadhrat (honorable) Isa, or Isa bin Marium, (Son of Mary), Nabi (Prophet) Isa, or al-Maseeh (Messiah).

Joel Richardson in his great book, *The Islamic Antichrist,* summarizes the activities of the Muslim Jesus upon his return to earth like this:

> 1. Jesus is said to return to the earth in the last days near a mosque in Damascus.
> 2. He will arrive at a time when the Mahdi and his army will be preparing to pray.
> 3. He will be asked to lead the prayer by the Mahdi, but will decline in direct deference to the Mahdi, whom Jesus declares to be the leader of the Muslims.
> 4. He will then pray behind the Mahdi as a subordinate.
> 5. He will be a faithful Muslim.
> 6. He will make a pilgrimage to Mecca.
> 7. He will visit Muhammad's grave and salute Muhammad, whereby Muhammad will return the salute from the grave.
> 8. He will destroy Christianity.
> 9. He will repeal the *jizyah* tax, which gave Jews and Christians permission to live in Muslim countries. When this tax is repealed, Jews and Christians have two options: convert to Islam or die.
> 10. He will establish Islamic *sharia* law throughout the entire earth.
> 11. He will kill the Antichrist (Dajjal) and his followers, made up largely of Jews and women.
> 12. He will remain on earth roughly forty years, during which time He will marry, have children, and then die.

The Muslim Jesus, in both his actions and nature, is far different from the biblical Jesus. Rather than coming to reign as King and Messiah over all the earth from Jerusalem, Jesus instead comes to convert the world to Islam or kill those who refuse to do so. Instead of coming to deliver faithful Christians and Jews, He comes instead to slaughter them.[1]

THE FALSE PROPHET AND THE MUSLIM JESUS

In our study thus far we have seen many things that startle the mind. There are so many similarities between Muslim eschatology found in the Hadith and Biblical eschatology found in the Bible. There are more amazing surprises yet to come. During the Tribulation Period and the reign of the Antichrist on earth we see that he has an accomplice, the False Prophet. We read about him in Revelation 13:11-18,

> *And I beheld another beast coming up out of the earth; and he had two horns like a lamb, and he spake as a dragon. And he exerciseth all the power of the first beast before him, and causeth the earth and them which dwell therein to worship the first beast, whose deadly wound was healed. And he doeth great wonders, so that he maketh fire come down from heaven on the earth in the sight of men, And deceiveth them that dwell on the earth by the means of those miracles which he had power to do in the sight of the beast; saying to them that dwell on the earth, that they should make an image to the beast, which had the wound by a sword, and did live. And he had power to give life unto the image of the beast, that the image of the beast should both speak, and cause that as many as would not worship the image of the beast should be killed. And he causeth all, both small and great, rich and poor, free and bond, to receive a mark in their right hand, or in their foreheads: And that no man might buy or sell, save he that had the mark, or the name of the beast, or the number of his name. Here is wisdom. Let him that hath understanding*

count the number of the beast: for it is the number of a man; and his number is Six hundred threescore and six.

Like the first beast, this second beast is a man possessed by Satan. He only has two horns (authority) compared to the Antichrist's ten horns. So he has less power. His power centers in religion and worship rather than in politics. Satan raises him up to bring the world to worship the Antichrist, his chosen one. To accomplish this, Satan lavishes on him speaking ability (*he spake as a dragon*), miraculous powers (*he maketh fire come down from heaven*), and the infamous system known as the mark of the beast. Only those wearing the mark of the beast (666) can sell or buy. The picture we get is that these two men under the possession of Satan are working together to lure men away from worshiping the God of the Bible.

As we meditate upon this unholy duet found in the Bible, another pair of men appears in Muslim traditions: the Mahdi and the Muslim Jesus. Just as the Antichrist was the key man and the False Prophet his sidekick, so the Mahdi is the head and the Muslim Jesus is his associate. As head, the Mahdi is the military man conquering country after country while the Muslim Jesus concerns himself with enforcing Islamic law or *sharia*. As his associate, He uses both persuasion and force. In his book, *The Approach of Armageddon?*, Kabbani writes:

> When Jesus returns he will personally correct the misrepresentation and misinterpretations about himself. He will affirm the true message that he brought the first time as a prophet, and that he never claimed to be the Son of God. Furthermore, he will reaffirm in his second coming what he prophesied in his first coming, bearing witness to the seal of the Messenger, Prophet Muhammad. In his second coming many non-Muslims will accept Jesus as a servant of Allah Almighty, as a Muslim and a member of the community of Muhammad.[2]

These two leaders, the False Prophet with the Antichrist and the Muslim Jesus with the Mahdi will enforce mass executions of all who will not submit to the Antichrist or to the Mahdi.

In concluding our remarks about Jesus in the Hadith, let me quote Joel Richardson, who said it so well:

> Muslims await a man who will claim to be Jesus Christ… If such a man ever exists, he will claim, according to Islamic tradition, that he has been alive in heaven for the past two thousand years, waiting to return to complete his life and accomplish his mission on earth. Such a man would be a liar—a true student of his master, the father of lies. He would come to fulfill what the Bible expresses to be the chief boiling desires of Satan: to either deceive Christians and Jews—indeed the entire earth—into worshipping him or to slaughter them. In the Bible, we see that it is for these very purposes that Satan will empower his False Prophet. The biblical description of the False Prophet and the Islamic description of the Muslim Jesus, on all the essential points, are identical.[3]

WHAT THE BIBLE SAYS ABOUT JESUS

Who is Jesus and what does the Bible say about Him? Dr. Charles Keen said it beautifully in his magazine, *The Unpublished Word*:

> In Genesis He is the Creator; in Exodus He is the Passover Lamb; in Leviticus He is the Atoning Blood; in Numbers He is the Smitten Rock; in Deuteronomy He is the Author of the Covenant.
>
> In Joshua He is the Scarlet Thread that Binds our hearts

in Christian love; in Judges He is the Great Deliverer; in Ruth He is Our Kinsman Redeemer; in 1 and 2 Samuel He is the Sweet Singer of Israel; in 1 and 2 Kings He is the Temple in the Holy of Holies; in 1 and 2 Chronicles He is Jesus the Promised King; in Ezra He is the Restorer of the backslider; in Nehemiah He is the Restorer of the Nation.

In Esther He is the Protector of His people; in Job He is Our Daysman who is Patient and Kind; in Psalms He is the Poet and the Shepherd; in Proverbs He is Wisdom; in Eccclesiastes He is the Teacher; in Song of Solomon He is Rose of Sharon, Lily of the Valley.

In Isaiah He is the Mighty God, the Prince of Peace, and yet the Suffering Savior; in Jeremiah He is the Balm of Gilead; in Lamentations He is the Weeping Prophet; in Ezekiel He is the Wheel in the middle of the wheel; in Daniel He is the Fourth man in the furnace; in Hosea He is the Faithful Husband; in Joel He is the Judge of the nations: in Amos He is Champion of social justice; in Obadiah the Deliverance on Mount Zion; in Jonah the God of the Second Chance; in Micah He is the Messiah of the Millennium; in Nahum He is the God of Vengeance; in Habakkuk He is the God of Justice; in Zephaniah He is the Day of the Lord; in Haggai He is the Restorer of order; in Zechariah He is the Great Branch; in Malachi He is the Sun of Righteousness rising with healing in His wings.

In Matthew He is King; in Mark He is Servant; in Luke He is Son of Man; in John He is Son of God; in Acts He is God the Holy Spirit; in Romans He is Grace; in 1 and 2 Corinthians He is the Giver of gifts; in Galatians He is the Fulfiller of the Law; in Ephesians He is the Head of the Body; in Philippians He is the Exalted One; in Colossians He is the Image of the Invisible God; in 1 and 2 Thessalonians He is Our Blessed Hope; in 1 and 2 Timothy He is the Bishop of our souls; in Titus He is the True elder; in

Philemon He is the Settler of our account; in Hebrews He is the Eternal Sacrifice; in James He is our Great Healer; in 1 and 2 Peter He is the Chief Cornerstone and the Returning Lord; in 1,2 and 3 John He is Our Strength and our Supply; in Jude He is the One who is able to keep you from falling; in Revelation He is King of Kings and Lord of Lords.[4]

The Bible is very clear as to who Jesus is and His purposes for coming to earth. Let us look at some of them.

Jesus will crush the serpent's (Satan) head. Genesis 3:15, *"And I will put enmity between thee and the woman, and between thy seed and her seed; it shall bruise thy head, and thou shalt bruise his heel."*

Jesus will save His people from their sins. Matthew 1:21, *"And she shall bring forth a son, and thou shalt call his name JESUS: for he shall save his people from their sins."*

Jesus will seek and save those who are lost. Luke 19:10, *"For the Son of man is come to seek and to save that which was lost."*

Jesus came to give eternal life to all who believe in Him. John 3:16, *"For God so loved the world, that he gave his only begotten Son, that whosoever believeth in him should not perish, but have everlasting life."*

Jesus came to reveal God, the Father. John 1:18, *"No man hath seen God at any time; the only begotten Son, which is in the bosom of the Father, he hath declared him."*

Jesus became poor that we might become rich. 2 Corinthians 8:9, *"For ye know the grace of our Lord Jesus Christ, that, though he was rich, yet for your sakes he became poor, that ye through his poverty might be rich."*

Jesus suffered that He might bring us to God. 1 Peter 3:18, *"For Christ also hath once suffered for sins, the just for the unjust, that he might bring us to God..."*

Jesus came to destroy the works of the devil. 1 John 3:8, *"... For this purpose the Son of God was manifested, that he might destroy the works of the devil."*

Jesus will defeat His enemies and will cast the Antichrist and False Prophet into the Lake of Fire. Revelation 19:19,20,

> *And I saw the beast, and the kings of the earth, and their armies, gathered together to make war against him that sat on the horse, and against his army. And the beast was taken, and with him the false prophet that wrought miracles before him, with which he deceived them that had received the mark of the beast, and them that worshipped his image. These both were cast alive into a lake of fire burning with brimstone.*

Jesus will cast Satan into the Lake of Fire. Revelation 20:10, *"And the devil that deceived them was cast into the lake of fire and brimstone, where the beast and the false prophet are, and shall be tormented day and night for ever and ever."*

Jesus will create a new heaven and a new earth. Revelation 21:1, *"And I saw a new heaven and a new earth: for the first heaven and the first earth were passed away; and there was no more sea."*

Without the ability to choose, we are nothing but robots. God did not create robots but creatures made in His image with the responsibility of making choices. God has given people choices. First, people can choose to believe the Koran and the Hadith and follow Mohammed and the Mahdi who will eventually come. Second, they can choose to believe the Bible and accept Jesus Christ as Lord and Savior. Third, they can choose to follow some other religion or to follow none. Inevitably, consequences follow choices. I urge you to take the words of God spoken to Moses seriously. Deuteronomy 30:19,20,

> *I call heaven and earth to record this day against you, that I have set before you life and death, blessing and cursing: therefore choose life, that both thou and thy seed may live: That thou mayest love the LORD thy God, and that thou mayest*

obey his voice, and that thou mayest cleave unto him: for he is thy life, and the length of thy days: that thou mayest dwell in the land which the LORD sware unto thy fathers, to Abraham, to Isaac, and to Jacob, to give them.obey his voice, and that thou mayest cleave unto him: for he is thy life, and the length of thy days: that thou mayest dwell in the land which the LORD sware unto thy fathers, to Abraham, to Isaac, and to Jacob, to give them.

CHAPTER NINE

DAJJAL: MONSTER OR SAVIOR?

Up to this point the Dajjal has been mentioned several times. Those unfamiliar with Muslim eschatology need to know that the Dajjal, the enemy of Islam, plays a major role in the end time's scenario. So who is he? According to Hadith traditions his name is Al-Maseeh the Messiah. Ad-Dajjal is his Arabic name. He will oppose the Mahdi and the Muslim Jesus in their efforts to impose Islam on the world. Dajjal is the name given in the Hadith to certain religious impostors who shall appear in the world; a term equivalent to the Christian use of the word antichrist. The Masihu 'd-Dajjal or "the lying Christ" is said to be the last of the Dajjals. He is the false Jewish Messiah and will be the only hope for Jewish survival.[1]

DAJJAL DESCRIBED

According to all the traditions, the Masih Dajjal has a blind eye, curly hair and also something wrong with his foot. A very unsavory character, indeed! The Masih Dajjal will first say that he is a prophet and then God. He will have a hell fire and a paradise by his side and people that refuse to follow him, will be forced to enter the hell-fire. However, this hell-fire will be an illusion and in reality will be cool and safe. The word *"kafir"* (unbeliever, infidel) will appear between his eyes. He will travel at great speeds, conveyed by a huge white mule. He will be known as the great deceiver who would deceive all humanity. The Dajjal will possess miraculous powers such as wiping his hand over the sick to heal them and raising the dead. By his powers he leads people down the path to hell. He will pretend to be the Messiah and deceive people by showing them amazing powers.[2]

THE LAST WAR

Dajjal will remain on the Earth for a period of forty days, of which the first day will be as long as a year, the second day as long as a month, the third as a week and the rest will be normal in length. He will try to gain entry to the two holy cities of Makkah and Madinah, but the angels who guard them will bar him from them. From there, he will flee to Syria, where he will meet resistance from the forces of Imam Mahdi, the leader of the Muslims. Then the battle between Good and Evil will begin in earnest.[3]

This Muslim tradition refers to the battle mentioned in Zechariah 12:10, and 14:1-4,

> *And I will pour upon the house of David, and upon the inhabitants of Jerusalem, the spirit of grace and of supplications: and they shall look upon me whom they have pierced, and they shall mourn for him, as one mourneth for his only son, and shall be in bitterness for him, as one that is in bitterness for his firstborn.*

Then Zechariah 14:1-4 describes the battle,

> *Behold, the day of the LORD cometh, and thy spoil shall be divided in the midst of thee. For I will gather all nations against Jerusalem to battle; and the city shall be taken, and the houses rifled, and the women ravished; and half of the city shall go forth into captivity, and the residue of the people shall not be cut off from the city.*
> *Then shall the LORD go forth, and fight against those nations, as when he fought in the day of battle. And his feet shall*

stand in that day upon the mount of Olives, which is before Jerusalem on the east, and the mount of Olives shall cleave in the midst thereof toward the east and toward the west, and there shall be a very great valley; and half of the mountain shall remove toward the north, and half of it toward the south.

According to the biblical account, Christ reveals Himself to the bewildered Jews who were suffering a terrible defeat and fights for them. Romans 11:26 tells the outcome of the battle: *"And so all Israel shall be saved: as it is written, There shall come out of Sion the Deliverer, and shall turn away ungodliness from Jacob."*

WORDS OF AN OPTIMISTIC MUSLIM

Muslims believe in a final battle, but to them the outcome is completely different. When asked what Muslims believe about the end of the world and Jesus' part in it, Muslim apologist Osama Abdallah gave an astonishing reply:

> Briefly, Christians believe that Jesus will come down to earth and fight for the state of Israel…What seems to be quite ironic to me is that those Jews that Jesus is supposedly going to fight for don't even believe in Jesus as GOD himself nor as a Messenger of GOD…Jesus never liked the Jews…Now without being biased, we Muslims have a story that makes a lot more sense and is empty of contradictions! We believe that Jesus will come down to earth toward the end of the world to fight the army of Satan which will be mostly from the "bad" Jews or "Zionist Jews" as we call them today, and the deceived Polytheist Christians, or the Trinitarian Christians, and the Pagan Polytheists, such as Hindus, Buddhists, etc…Some Jews and many Christians will be among the good and blessed who will fight

with Jesus' (Muslim Jesus) side. The army of Satan will be led by a person who will claim to be Jesus Christ himself. The Muslims will call him the Dajjal or the Deceiver. The real Jesus' army will fight the Dajjal's army and defeat him. The empire of Israel will fall and the religion of Islam will prevail.[4]

JESUS' SECOND COMING ACCORDING TO THE HADITH

The Hadith records Isa, i.e., Jesus' return and the events associated with it:

He will descend on Mount Afeeq, on the white Eastern Minaret of Damascus. He will descend from the heavens with his hands resting on the shoulders of two angels. His cheeks will be flat and his hair straight. When he lowers his head it will seem as if water is flowing from his hair, when he raises his head, it will appear as though his hair is beaded with silvery pearls. He will descend during the time of Fajr and the leader of the Muslims will address him thus, 'O`Roohullah, lead the salat.' (prayer). Isa (Jesus - peace be upon him) will decline with the words, 'The virtue of this Ummah is that they lead each other.

The import of these words is that Jesus recognizes the Mahdi as the real leader of Islam.

After the prayer, Isa (Jesus - peace be upon him) will prepare himself to do battle and shall take up a spear. An army shall return from a campaign launched before the arrival of Isa (Jesus - peace be upon him). They shall bring glad tidings of victory over India, granted to them by the Lord Almighty. Isa (Jesus - peace be upon him) shall set out in pursuit of Dajjal.

All those who embraced the evil of Dajjal shall perish even as the breath of Isa (Jesus - peace be upon him) touches them. The breath of Isa (Jesus - peace be upon him) shall precede him as far as the eye can see. Dajjal will be captured at Lydda. The Dark Messiah shall begin to melt, as lead melts in fire. The spear of Isa (Jesus - peace be upon him) shall plunge into Dajjal's chest, ending his dreaded reign. The followers of Dajjal will be rooted out, for even the trees and rocks will speak out against them. Then all battles shall cease and the world will know an age of peace. Then truly the sheep will lie in the shadow of the wolf without fear. The rule of Jesus will be just and all shall flock to him to enter the folds of the one true religion, Islam.[5]

A study of Muslim traditions reveals how satanic Islam really is. At his return, the Muslim Jesus repudiates his former ministry. In the *Signs of the Qiyamma* (final judgment) Shafi and Usmani, two well-respected Islamic scholars, vigorously insist that Jesus did not die and is not the Son of God. They write:

> Jesus will confirm that he is alive and has not died and he is not the Son of God but [merely] His [Allah's] slave and Messenger, and Isa [Jesus] will testify against those who had called him son of God, the Christians, and those who belied him, the Jews.[6]

Sheik Kabbani, chairman of the Islamic Supreme Council of America, makes the Muslim Jesus' role very clear:

> Like all prophets, Prophet Jesus came with the divine message of surrender to God Almighty, which is Islam.... Jesus will personally correct the misrepresentations and misinterpretations about himself. He will affirm the true message he brought in his time as a prophet, and that he

never claimed to be the son of God. Furthermore, he will reaffirm in his second coming what he prophesied in his first coming, bearing witness to the seal of the Messenger, Prophet Muhammad. In his second coming many non-Muslims will accept Jesus as a servant of Allah Almighty, as a Muslim, and a member of the community of Muhammad.[7]

A well-known tradition lays out very clearly the ministry of the Muslim Jesus. He will break all the crosses, kill all the swine, abolish the jizyah tax (a Muslim tax levied on Christians to keep them from being killed), and kill the Muslim Antichrist (Dajjal) and his followers.[8] Islam is the devil's masterpiece, and except for the power of our sovereign Lord, the whole world would fall under the rule of Sharia, the Koran.

The picture is clear. We have noted that there are two books: the Bible and the Koran; two Saviors: Jesus Christ and Mohammed; two returning deliverers: The Mahdi and the Lord Jesus Christ; two evil ones: the Dajjal and the Antichrist; two assistants: the Muslim Jesus and the False Prophet. These similarities of the eschatology of the Bible and the Muslim traditions stagger the imagination.

SIGNS OF THE END

Both the Hadith traditions and the Bible give signs of the last days. First let us look at the signs from the Hadith. The following are signs of the forthcoming of Dajjal:

People will stop offering prayers
Dishonesty will be the way of life
Falsehood will become a virtue
People will mortgage their faith for worldly gains
Usury and bribery will become legitimate

Imbeciles would rule over the wise
Blood of innocents would be shed
Pride will be taken on acts of oppression
The rulers will be corrupt
The scholars will be hypocrites
Adultery will be rampant
Women will dress like men, and men will dress like women
The liars and the treacherous will be respected
There will be acute famine at the time[8]

The Bible gives these signs in 2 Timothy 3:1-4. *"This know also, that in the last days perilous times shall come.*

> *For men shall be lovers of their own selves*
> *covetous*
> *boasters*
> *proud*
> *blasphemers*
> *disobedient to parents*
> *unthankful*
> *unholy*
> *without natural affection*
> *trucebreakers, false accusers*
> *incontinent*
> *fierce*
> *despisers of those that are good*
> *traitors*
> *heady*
> *highminded*
> *lovers of pleasures more than lovers of God*
> *having a form of godliness, but denying the power thereof: from such turn away.*

Muslims have full confidence that the Mahdi and the Muslim

Jesus will save them, destroy Christianity and Judaism, and usher in Islam's golden age. Christians, born of the Spirit and washed in the blood, are more than confident the prophecies of the Word of God will be fulfilled. My faith is in Jesus Christ. I believe without fear the truth of 2 Thessalonians 1:7-10,

> *And to you who are troubled rest with us, when the Lord Jesus shall be revealed from heaven with his mighty angels, In flaming fire taking vengeance on them that know not God, and that obey not the gospel of our Lord Jesus Christ: Who shall be punished with everlasting destruction from the presence of the Lord, and from the glory of his power; When he shall come to be glorified in his saints, and to be admired in all them that believe (because our testimony among you was believed) in that day.*

CHAPTER TEN
ANTICHRIST'S EMPIRE - EAST OR WEST

Changes, changes, changes! The concept of change won the presidency for Barak Obama. As mentioned before, the most astonishing event of the last fifty years has been the rise and ascendancy of Islam. Changes that Bible prophecy teachers of fifty years ago never dreamed possible, i.e., the possibility of an Islamic Caliphate uniting all fifty odd Islamic nations of the world.

Also, along side the rise of Islam, the diminishing of the power and influence of Europe, namely the European Union, cannot be denied. The countries of Europe are toothless, that is, they have no mighty armies to enforce their will in the world. The future of Europe is not encouraging. More will be said about Europe's demise later in the book.

These changes force the serious Bible teacher to review his premises. Every logical argument has a premise and a conclusion. If the premise, a proposition antecedently supposed or proved, (Webster's New Collegiate Dictionary) happens to be incorrect then the conclusion will also be incorrect. It does not give me joy to go against the opinion of those that I love and admire. I believe the suppositions, the theories, and the surmising of most of our prophecy teachers have been wrong. In this chapter, which will not be easy, I will put forth what I believe are the correct premises which will lead to the correct conclusion. I must hasten to say that I do not set forth myself as a prophecy expert, but as a lifelong student of the Bible, a student of Islam, of current affairs, and as an avid seeker of truth, I do read, study, and examine the writings of the experts. Over the course of my long ministry of fifty-nine years, I have made it a practice to read, read, and read. If a prophecy teacher shows that his premises or presuppositions are more logical and that the conclusion he reaches is in accordance with biblical prophecy, then I follow truth. All those who love the truth follow the truth.

Ravi Zacharias says there are two tests for truth: correspondence and coherence. That which is true must correspond to facts, to reality. Coherence means that truth will be reasonable, logical.[1] In our discussion we will seek to adhere to these two principles. So, if anyone after carefully studying this chapter disagrees with my conclusions we will still be friends. I welcome all facts and information that adheres to the truth. And once again I want to emphasize that it causes me pain to contradict those I love and respect. But as a teacher of the Word of God I have an obligation to find the truth and teach the truth.

NATIONS COMPOSING ANTICHRIST'S EMPIRE

From our rather extensive study of the Antichrist and the similarities between the biblical Antichrist and the Muslim Mahdi, to me at least, it is evident that the Antichrist will be a Muslim. If the Antichrist is a Muslim it follows that his empire will be an Islamic empire. This is an example of coherence, i.e., the conclusion must be reasonable. As we examine the nations mentioned in the Bible that will come up against Israel, they all are Islamic nations. Despite the numerous prevailing arguments for the emergence of a revived European Roman Empire out of which emerges the Antichrist, none of the countries the Bible mentions are European but rather Islamic. In times past, some prophecy teachers predicted that Islam as a religion would fade away and become irrelevant in the end times. Undeniably, Islam will not fade away but with the passing of time will play an even more dominant role in prophetical events.

GOG AND MAGOG

The Prophet Ezekiel lists the nations of this final Antichrist Empire that will attack Israel. Ezekiel 38:1 says,

> *And the word of the LORD came unto me, saying, Son of man, set thy face against Gog, the land of Magog, the chief prince of Meshech and Tubal, and prophesy against him, And say, Thus saith the Lord GOD; Behold, I am against thee, O Gog, the chief prince of Meshech and Tubal: And I will turn thee back, and put hooks into thy jaws, and I will bring thee forth, and all thine army, horses and horsemen, all of them clothed with all sorts of armour, even a great company with bucklers and shields, all of them handling swords:* **Persia**, **Ethiopia**, *and* **Libya** *with them; all of them with shield and helmet:* **Gomer**, *and all his bands; the house of* **Togarmah** *of the north quarters, and all his bands: and many people with thee. Be thou prepared, and prepare for thyself, thou, and all thy company that are assembled unto thee, and be thou a guard unto them.*

To properly understand this passage we must carefully identify the leader and the nations involved in this coalition against Israel. First, let us identify Gog and Magog. Gog is a title such as king or pharaoh. Hence, Gog is the leader of the land of Magog. There are two mentions of Gog; one is here in Ezekiel and the other is Revelation 20:7-10. Notice what the Apostle John writes,

> *And when the thousand years are expired, Satan shall be loosed out of his prison, And shall go out to deceive the nations which are in the four quarters of the earth,* **Gog** *and* **Magog***, to gather them together to battle: the number of whom is as the sand of the sea. And they went up on the breadth of the earth, and compassed the camp of the saints about, and the*

> *beloved city: and fire came down from God out of heaven, and devoured them. And the devil that deceived them was cast into the lake of fire and brimstone, where the beast and the false prophet are, and shall be tormented day and night for ever and ever.*

Traditionally, prophecy teachers have identified Gog, not as the Antichrist, but as another leader of Russia who brings a coalition against Israel.

Joel Richardson in *Islamic Antichrist* gives two reasons why the two Gogs mentioned are both the same. First, the second Gog and Magog appear at the end of the millennium gathering to once again attack Jerusalem. Since they share the same names as Gog and Magog mentioned in Ezekiel why are they not the same. Obviously, the two Gogs and Magogs share more than a name, and there is a definite correlation between the two. Gog, (Antichrist) the leader, and Magog his fellow countrymen and a coalition of Muslim nations attacked Jerusalem at the end of the Tribulation. This was the battle of Armageddon. At the end of the Millennium another Gog and Magog appear. This Gog (king) is an instrument of the devil to lead a final rebellion against the God of heaven. Those that see Gog and Antichrist as two separate entities must explain why the two have the same name but yet are not the same.[2]

Keep in mind who the Antichrist really is. He is the Devil incarnate; he is the Devil's puppet, who shares worship as it were with his father, the Devil. Just as Satan raised up Gog in Ezekiel, he will also raise up a Gog in a final rebellion against God. Both of these rebellions are led by a person named Gog. Satan is the instigator of both. Why complicate matters by inventing two Gogs?

Second, Ezekiel pointedly says that the prophets before him spoke of Gog. It is important to remember that this is in the context of Gog attacking Jerusalem. Ezekiel 38:17 says, *Thus saith the Lord GOD; Art thou he*[Gog] *of whom I have spoken in* **old time** *by my servants the prophets of Israel, which prophesied in those days many years* *that I would bring thee against them?"* You will look in vain to find any references specifically of Gog and Magog but there are abundant passages in the prophets before Ezekiel describing Antichrist and his armies attacking Israel. Later these passages will be pointed out.[3]

If Gog is the Antichrist then what is Magog? Walid Shoebat quotes *The Schaff-Herzog Encyclopedia of Religious Knowledge*, citing ancient Assyrian writings, places the location of Magog in the land mass between ancient Armenia and Media—in short, the republics south of Russia and north of Israel, comprised of Azerban, Afghanistan, Turkestan, Chechnya, Turkey, Iran, and Dagestan. Significantly, all of them are Muslim nations.[4]

Matthew Henry in his *Complete Commentary on the Whole Bible* says, "Some think they find them [Gog and Magog] afar off, in Scythia, Tartary, and [southern] Russia. Others think they find them nearer the land of Israel, in Syria, and Asia the Less [Turkey]."[5] So to answer the question what is Magog? It is a large land mass north of Israel and south of Russia. From this area, Gog, the leader of Magog will lead his army. Note that all these countries, whether in southern Russia or in Turkey, they are still all Islamic countries.

THE NORTHERN CONFEDERATION

At this time we will discuss a very important matter, the Northern Confederation. According to the majority of prophecy teachers the army attacking Jerusalem in Ezekiel 38 is led by the modern country of Russia. I believe this is a false premise and upon this false premise the great majority of Bible prophecy teachers build their case. Dr. C.I. Scofield in his famous reference Bible popularized this view in his notes on Ezekiel 38:2, 3.

That the primary reference is to the northern (European)

powers, headed up by Russia, all agree. The whole passage should be read in connection with Zechariah 12:1-4; 14:1-9; Matthew 24:14-39; Revelation 14:14-29; 19:17-21. "Gog" is the prince of "Magog" his land. The reference to Meshech and Tubal (Moscow and Tobolsk) is a clear mark of identification. Russia and the northern powers have been the latest persecutors of dispersed Israel, and it is congruous both with the divine justice and with the covenants (e.g. Genesis 15:18, note Deuteronomy 30:3, note) that destruction should fall at the climax of the last mad attempt to exterminate the remnant of Israel in Jerusalem. The whole prophecy belongs to the yet future "day of Jehovah" (Isaiah 2:10-22; Revelation 19:11-21, and to the battle of Armageddon (Revelation 16:14; 19:19, note), but includes the final revolt of the nations at the close of the Kingdom-age (Revelation 20:7-9).[6]

If we refer to some of the greatest Biblical references, like *Oxford Bible Atlas*, and *The Moody Atlas of Bible Lands*, they all locate Magog, Meshech, Tubal, Gomer, and Beth Togarmah in Asia Minor, and not Russia. In our test for truth here we have correspondence. Does the premise adhere to fact? By presupposing that the land of Magog is modern day Russia and the cities of Meschech and Tubal are the Russian cities of Moscow and Tubolsk, the presupposition is not true because it does not adhere to facts.

Walid Shoebat argues against the Russian connection in this way:

> Another important point is that Meshech and Tubal must be tied to Magog, yet these are in Asia Minor and not Russia. Magog is specifically referred to as the region of "the land of Magog, chief prince (head or ruler of) of Meshech and Tubal." (Ezekiel 38:2) Because Meshech and Tubal are regions of Turkey—Magog must be related to Turkey.

Otherwise the passage would make little sense. How could Russia be the head over regions of Turkey? It makes better sense to conclude that Gog is a leader from the land of Magog and the leader of Meshech and Tubal, all of which are in Turkey. When it comes to the geographical location of Meshech and Tubal, you will never find a serious historian, Bible dictionary or Bible map that would agree with any of the proponents for a Russian location. The error of the Russian theory arose from the Scofield Study Bible, which identifies Meshech and Tubal with the modern Russian cities of Moscow and Tobolsk. The only basis for this interpretation is the somewhat similar sound of the two words. Thus: Meshech sounds like Moscow, and Tubal sounds like Tobolsk. However, one cannot simply take a word from an ancient Semitic language (in this case Hebrew) and find a correlation to a modern name from a drastically different language (in this case an early form of Scandinavian) simply because the two words "sound the same." While this may be convincing to some from the sole reason of phonetics, it is very irresponsible hermeneutics.[7]

ARMAGEDDON

Many Bible prophecy teachers teach that the invading coalition of nations described in Ezekiel 38-39 is not the army of Antichrist, but of another army led by an evil world leader from Russia who is destroyed by Christ prior to Christ's defeat of the Antichrist. This is the premise or the presupposition of those who teach the Northern Confederation is the army attacking Jerusalem at this time.

The presupposition I put forth is that the battle for Jerusalem in Revelation 19 and the battle for Jerusalem in Ezekial 38 are the same battle. Let us see how the two battles are so similar. In both battles—Gog (Ezekiel) and Armageddon (Revelation)—Christ is present. Ezekiel 38:20 says, "... *all the men that are upon the face of the earth, shall shake at **my** presence, and the mountains shall be thrown down, and the steep places shall fall, and every wall shall fall to the ground.*" The presence of Christ is made more specific in Ezekiel 39:7 *"And the heathen shall know that I am Jehovah, the Holy One **in** Israel.* Not the holy One **of** Israel but the holy One **in** Israel. Jehovah (Jesus) is actually present in Israel with His people. Christ's presence in the battle described in Revelation has Him on a white horse leading the armies of heaven (raptured saints) to battle to save Jerusalem.

Second, in both battles there is an earthquake. Ezekiel 38:19 says, "... *and all the men that are upon the face of the earth, shall **shake** at my presence, and the **mountains shall be thrown down**, and the steep **places shall fall**, and every wall* shall fall to the ground." Revelation 16:19,20 says,

> *And the great city was divided into three parts, and the cities of the nations fell: and great Babylon came in remembrance before God, to give unto her the cup of the wine of the fierceness of his wrath. And every island fled away, and the mountains were not found.*

Third, in both battles there is a call for the birds to come and feast. At Armageddon Revelation 19:17 says, *"And I saw an angel standing in the sun; and he cried with a loud voice, saying to all the fowls that fly in the midst of heaven, Come and gather yourselves together unto the supper of the great God."* At the battle of Gog, Ezekiel 39:17 says,

> *And, thou son of man, thus saith the Lord GOD; Speak unto every feathered fowl, and to every beast of the field, Assemble yourselves, and come; gather yourselves on every side to my sacrifice that I do sacrifice for you, even a great sacrifice upon the mountains of Israel, that ye may eat flesh, and drink blood.*

> *Ye shall eat the flesh of the mighty, and drink the blood of the princes of the earth, of rams, of lambs, and of goats, of bullocks, all of them fatlings of Bashan. And ye shall eat fat till ye be full, and drink blood till ye be drunken, of my sacrifice which I have sacrificed for you. Thus ye shall be filled at my table with horses and chariots, with mighty men, and with all men of war, saith the Lord GOD.*

I could go on and list several more similarities but I think the point has been made that the two battles being described are the same. One last argument and perhaps the strongest proving Gog and Antichrist are the same and the battle in Ezekiel 38, 39 and the battle in Revelation 16, 19 are the same is given by Walid Shoebat in this statement:

> Perhaps the strongest argument that Gog is Antichrist is that whenever the direction from which Antichrist coming is mentioned, it is always the north, and never the European west. Yet, there isn't a single verse in Scripture mentioning a European invasion. You can try. It simply doesn't exist. Yet people cling to the theory of western invasion developed from allegories in Revelation and Daniel. Western prophecy analysts have always argued that the Antichrist comes from Western Europe without providing a single text from the Bible as evidence.[8]

I would like to give a personal word of testimony at this point. For many years I have read Ezekiel 38 and heard of the Northern Confederation, consisting of Russia and her allies, but this theory never seemed true to me. It lacked solid biblical proof and as we have seen it was based on a false premise. When I began to study Walid Shoebat's *God's War on Terror — Islam, Prophecy and the Bible*, I knew, at last, I had found the truth. I spent at least forty hours carefully reading this book. My whole outlook on the end times finally came into focus.

Then later I discovered Joel Richardson's *The Islamic Antichrist – The Shocking Truth about the Real Nature of the Beast* which confirmed in my mind and heart that I had found the answers I had been looking for concerning Islam and the end times. I am deeply indebted to these men for their scholarship, research, and gift of making difficult subjects understandable. Lest someone think I am following men I assure you that every statement they make is weighed to see if it agrees with the Word of God, corresponds to fact, and is coherent, i.e., reasonable. I am aware that many people in our circles will never bother to purchase a large expensive book by a person they do not know. And to someone not vitally interested in the subject, the reading of such could become tedious. As I mentioned before, I am not an expert on prophecy, but I am vitally interested to study the writings of those who know their Bible and are able to communicate God's plan for the end times. So my purpose is to digest what these men have written and distill their findings in simple, easy to understand style. My motivation is to communicate truth because I believe what Jesus said: *"Ye shall know the truth and the truth shall make you free"* (John 8:32).

CHAPTER ELEVEN
ROME OR ISLAM

At the beginning of the last chapter I said it would not be easy. Well, neither is this chapter going to be easy. We have dealt with one false premise, the Northern Confederation of which the modern nation of Russia will be the head. Now we come to another premise that practically all prophetic Bible teachers hold tenaciously: the last empire, the legs of iron and the feet partly of iron and partly of clay is the Roman Empire and the ten toes are the ten countries in the revived Roman Empire. Dr. Zomaya Solomon in his fine book, *The Beast and the End Times,* gives the classic and accepted view of most prophecy teachers.

> Daniel delves deeply into the interpretation of the Fourth World Empire, the Roman Empire. Daniel mentions that it is a strong power that subdues all things after breaking every resistance that arises. The prophet talks about the 'ten toes' made up of clay and of iron to signify the dual nature of the kingdom: 'partly strong and partly broken' (Daniel 2:42b). Then Daniel provides another description of the Fourth Empire. The iron and the clay, Daniel says, 'shall not cleave to one another' (Daniel 2:43b). As the Revived Roman Empire begins to come together at the end of time, which it appears, it is taking place nowadays, it will not stick together wholeheartedly.. It is made of weak material: 'partly strong, and partly broken.'[1]

THE FOURTH EMPIRE IS THE ISLAMIC EMPIRE

I would ask the reader to be patient and follow the line of arguments that has convinced me that Rome is not the Fourth Empire, but the Islamic Empire, beginning with Mohammed and ending in the Ottoman Empire.

The Islamic Empire began with Mohammed (570-622 A.D.) in Arabia and through his caliphs (leaders of the caliphate) spread from India in the east to Spain in the west. The Muslims captured Jerusalem in the 600s A.D. The Islamic Empire gradually evolved into the Ottoman Empire.

Since most of us know next to nothing about the Ottoman Empire, let me fill in a few details. It was a vast Turkish sultanate of southwest Asia, northeast Africa, and southeast Europe. It was founded in the 13th century by Osman I and ruled by his descendants until its dissolution after World War I. Originally a small state controlled by Ottoman or Osmani Turks, it spread rapidly, superseding the Byzantine (Greek) Empire in the east. It was an empire that lasted from 1299 to 1922. It was succeeded by the Republic of Turkey, which was officially proclaimed on October 29, 1923. At its zenith, the Ottoman Empire was huge and powerful. It came close to conquering Vienna, Austria in 1600's. The sultans, heads of state, were also known as caliphs who were the heads of the Islamic Caliphate. In 1453 Mehmet II conquered Constantinople and renamed it Istanbul.[2]

In Nebuchadnezzar's dream, each component of the statue represents a kingdom or an empire that will succeed its predecessor. It is admitted that the prevailing position throughout history by Jewish and Christian interpreters has been that the dream portrays the following four kingdoms: Babylon, Medo-Persia, Greece, and Rome. Please bear with me as I give support to the presupposition that the fourth empire was not Rome but the Islamic/Ottoman Empire.

ROME NEVER CONQUERED NEBUCHADNEZZAR'S EMPIRE

While Rome was a dominant force in world history, its effect upon the Mesopotamian region was minimal. It was never able to secure control over the regions east of the Euphrates River. In 117 A.D., shortly before the death of Trajan, he and his Roman troops made incursions into portions of Mesopotamia, but Roman rule was never established there. Because Nebuchadnezzar's dream covered a period of thirteen hundred years, the Roman Empire is only a footnote in Babylonian/Mesopotamian history, and thus it was not emphasized in Nebuchadnezzar's dream.

The primary empires that would conquer and rule over Babylon were all laid out consecutively. Daniel 2:40 says, *"There will be a fourth kingdom, strong as iron—for iron breaks and smashes everything—and iron breaks things to pieces, so it will crush and break all the others."* "All the others" refers to all the other kingdoms of Babylon, Medo-Persia, and Greece. Did Rome crush all the other empires mentioned above? The answer is no!"[3]

Justin's *History of the World* describes the battle between the Parthians, who ruled Mesopotamia, and the Romans:

> The Parthians, in whose hands the empire of the east now is, having divided the world, as it were, with the Romans, were originally exiled from Scythia…Being assailed by the Romans, also, in three wars, under the conduct of the greatest of generals, and at the most flourishing period of the republic, they alone, of all nations, were not only a match for them, but came off victorious.[4]

So we cannot say that Rome crushed the Babylonian or Medo-Persian Empires. Also, concerning the Greek Empire, Rome did control some of the territory conquered by Alexander the Great, but in the end the Hellenist culture conquered Rome. Thus neither can it be said that Rome "crushed" the Greek Empire.

ISLAM CONQUERS ALL

While Rome did not conquer all of the previous empires, the fourth empire of Daniel 2 accomplished this feat. The Islamic Empire fulfilled these requirements completely. Islam conquered all of the three previous empires – Babylonian, Medo-Persian, and Grecian. Islam also conquered the Roman Empire, which had ceased to exist in Europe.

Revelation 13:1-2 states that the fourth beast constitutes the three previous empires.

> *And I stood upon the sand of the sea, and saw a beast rise up out of the sea, having seven heads and ten horns, and upon his horns ten crowns, and upon his heads the name of blasphemy. And the beast which I saw was like unto a **leopard**, and his feet were as the feet of a **bear**, and his mouth as the mouth of a **lion:** and the dragon gave him his power, and his seat, and great authority.*

This, then, must exclude Europe. Islam conquered the entire Byzantine Roman Empire, which included Iraq (Babylon) and Iran (Persia), and large portions of what was the Western Roman Empire. Obviously, the Roman Empire cannot make this claim. Thus only Islam meets the biblical criterion.[5]

Our premise is that the four kingdoms or empires described in Nebuchadnezzar's dream are: Babylonian, Medo-Persian, Grecian or possibly Greco-Roman, and Islamic.

By the Islamic Empire is meant the various manifestations of the Islamic Caliphate, which culminated in the Ottoman Empire. This position is not unique. Among the well-known sages and rabbis who have held this view are Ibn Ezra, one of the most distinguished Jewish writers of the Middle Ages, and others of like fame. Ibn Ezra said:

> Rome is included in the third kingdom as relatives of the Greeks… The complete omission of the mighty and extensive Arab Kingdom is simply too big of an oversight that needs to be explained by those who hold to the Roman interpretation. The fourth kingdom is the Arab Muslim kingdom.[6]

Many historians see Rome as an extension of the Grecian Empire rather than a separate entity by itself. The Roman and Greek Empires in many ways are similar as they shared common borders, culture and language, as well as a common religion. It is also quite possible the Roman Empire is not even considered in the image.

NOT A NEW INTERPRETATION

Let the reader know that this interpretation has been held by Christian scholars ancient and recent.
John Wesley said:

> Indeed, the iron teeth closely match Islam. Ever since the religion of Islam appeared in the world, the espousers of it…have been as wolves and tigers to all other nations, rending and tearing all that fell into their merciless paws, and grinding them with iron teeth; that numberless cities are razed from the foundation, and only their names remaining; that many countries, which were once as the garden of God, are now a desolate wilderness; and that so many once numerous and powerful nations are vanished from the earth! Such was, and is at this day, the rage, the fury, the revenge of these destroyers of mankind.[7]

Sir Robert Anderson, one-time head of Scotland Yard and well-known author and Bible prophecy teacher, has this to say:

> It must be owned that there was nothing in the history of ancient Rome to correspond with the main characteristics of (the fourth) beast unless the symbolism used is to be very loosely interpreted. To 'devour the earth, tread it down and break it in pieces' is fairly descriptive of other empires, but Ancient Rome was precisely the one power that added government to conquer, and instead of treading down and breaking in pieces the nations it subdued, sought rather to mould them to its own civilization and polity…Now, Daniel 2 expressly names the Mediterranean ('the Great Sea') as the scene of the conflict between the four beasts. But there is no doubt that Egypt, Turkey, and Greece will be numbered among the ten kingdoms…To the scheme here indicated (the fourth empire is Islamic and not Roman) the objection may naturally be raised: Is it possible that the most powerful nations of the world, England, Germany, and Russia are to have no part in the great drama of the Last Days? But it must be remembered first, that the relative importance of the great Powers may be different at the time when these events shall be fulfilled, and secondly, that difficulties of this kind may depend entirely on the silence of Scripture, or, in other words, on our own ignorance…In the prophet's view (Daniel) the Levant (Middle East) and not the Adriatic (European), Jerusalem and not Rome, is the center of the world.[8]

Jonathan Edwards was well aware of Islam and its threat. In looking at the demonic locusts and horsemen in Revelation 9, Edwards saw a clear allusion to the Muslim armies. In referring to the False Prophet of Revelation 13 and the locusts and the horsemen of Revelation 9 Edwards says: "Here an eye seems to be had to Mahomet (Muhammad), whom his followers call the prophet of God."[9]

Edwards has more to say about the Islamic Empire:

> Satan's Mahometan (Muslim) Kingdom shall be utterly overthrown. The locusts and the horsemen in the ninth chapter of Revelation have their appointed time set there, and the false prophet shall be destroyed. And then—though Mahometanism has been so vastly propagated in the world, and is upheld by such a great empire—this smoke, which has ascended out of the bottomless pit, shall be utterly scattered before the light of that glorious day, and the Mahometan Empire shall fall at the sound of the great trumpet which shall be blown.[10]

Commenting on Edwards' remarks, Walid Shoebat makes an interesting observation:

> Edwards' comments about the locusts are rooted in the fact that in ancient history, Arabs were associated with locusts. Even the Hebrew word for 'locust" and "Arab" are almost identical. The Arab word for locust is Gindib. The Monolith of Shalmeneser III from Kurkuk, the oldest account from Babylon and the oldest document mentioning the Arabs, list Gi-in-di-bu' Ar-ba-a-a regarding Arabs and their territory called "Gindibu.[11]

The well-known late Catholic radio speaker, **Bishop Fulton Sheen,** in 1950 had this to say about Islam:

> Today (1950), the hatred of the Moslem countries against the West is becoming hatred against Christianity itself. Although the statesmen have not yet taken it into account,

there is still grave danger that the temporal power of Islam may return and, with it, the menace that it may shake off a West which has ceased to be Christian, and affirm itself as a great anti-Christian world power.[12]

His prediction has certainly been fulfilled.

DEMOGRAPHICS TELL THE STORY

In his book, *America Alone*, a New York Times best-seller which I read several years ago, Mark Steyn tells of the drastic changes facing Europe in the years ahead:

> In 1970, the developed nations (the non-Muslim majority nations of the world) had twice as big a share of the global population as the Muslim world: 30 percent to 15 percent. By 2000, they were at parity: each had 20 percent…The salient feature of Europe, Canada, Japan and Russia is that they are running out of babies. What's happening in the developed world is one of the fastest demographic evolutions in history…In other words; most of the developed non-Muslim nations are simply not having enough children to maintain their populations.
> Meanwhile Muslims are having far more children than any other group on the earth. It is only a matter of time then before many European nations are overrun by Middle-eastern and Northern African immigrants—and thus Islam…The number of Muslims in contemporary Europe is estimated at 50 million. It is expected to double in twenty years. By 2025, one third of all children will be born in Muslim families…In 2050, 60% of all Italians will have no brothers, no sisters, no cousins, no aunts, no uncles. The other 40% will be Muslim. By mid-century, the tiny

Muslim nation of Yemen will have a greater population than Russia, one of the largest countries in the world.

Seventeen European nations are now at what demographers call 'lowest-low' fertility: 1.3 births per woman. In theory, those countries will find their population halving every thirty-five years or so. In practice, it will be much quicker than that, as the savvier youngsters figure there's no point in sticking around a country that turned into an undertaker's waiting room... Consider these statistics regarding the percentage of the population under the age of fifteen: Spain and Germany 14%, the United Kingdom 18%, the United States 21%, and Saudi Arabia 39%, Pakistan 42%, and Yemen 47%.[13]

These statistics send a chill down our spines. The sadness of the situation was caught in Henryk M. Broder's article in the *Brussels Journal*, "The Rape of Europe," in which he says, "Young Europeans who love freedom better emigrate. Europe as we know it will no longer exist 20 years from now."[14]

Two premises or presuppositions have been made in this chapter. First, the majority view's premise is that the Antichrist will come from Rome and the Antichrist's kingdom will be a Western or European coalition. Second, the minority view – though as we have seen, it is not a novel view — is that the Antichrist will be a Muslim and the fourth empire of Nebuchadnezzar's statue is the Islamic Empire.

Remember our truth test. First, there must be correspondence to fact. Three compelling facts make it difficult for me to believe that Rome, a revived Roman Empire, is the fourth beast of Nebuchadnezzar's image. First, Rome did not conquer the three previous empires. The countries east of the Euphrates River repelled the Romans and were never conquered. Second, the nature of the Roman Empire does not match the description that it is a strong power that subdues all things after breaking every resistance that arises. Rome was a builder, not a destroyer, of nations. Third, demographics, the statistical study of populations as to births, marriages, mortality and health, prove in a shocking way that Europe and the Roman Empire are not in a state of revival, but will soon fade away. These facts cannot be ignored. Truth is defined as that which corresponds to fact. If that be so, I cannot see how the fourth beast could be Rome.

The second truth test is coherence or reasonableness. The ascendancy of Islam and the descendancy of Europe and the Catholic Church make it unreasonable to believe the premise that the fourth beast is Rome.

On the other hand, if we put the truth test to the premise that the fourth beast is the Islamic Empire, in my opinion, it will pass both the correspondence test and the coherence test. First, the Islamic Empire, beginning with Mohammed and culminating in the Ottoman Empire, did indeed conquer the three previous empires. If our premise is correct, the third empire was the Greco-Roman Empire. In 1453 Mehmet II, Caliph of the Ottoman Empire captured Constantinople and thus destroyed the Greco-Roman Empire as predicted by Daniel and portrayed in Nebuchadnezzar's image.

Second, a study of Islam proves that it is a strong power that subdues all things after breaking every resistance that arises. The nature and the activities of Islam fit exactly the description of the fierceness and cruelty of this empire. History books have overlooked Islam's expansion into India, in which millions upon millions of idolaters were slaughtered.

Third, the present reality of a revived Islam — funded by billions of petro dollars and motivated by radical Islamists who want to impose their creed and cruelty upon the whole world — cannot be denied. So the premise of the fourth empire being Islamic passes the correspondence test, i.e., it corresponds to the facts involved.

And then it passes the coherence test in that this premise is reasonable. With Islam ascending and Europe descending, how is it reasonable to believe a liberal Europe, which does not practice capital punishment, without a strong military, overrun by Muslim immigrants, will be that last empire? The last empire will be fierce, bloodthirsty, beheaders of all who resist, with a military force that will conquer the world? Does the European Union have those ambitions? I think not. Looking at the situation in the world today, it is not reasonable to believe that the European Union will result in a coalition of ten countries which are the ten toes of the statue in Nebuchadnezzar's image.

While that scenario is not reasonable, it seems quite reasonable that Islam fits the bill. Its plans for a Caliphate (Muslim government) with ten entities uniting all the Islamic nations, is in the process of formation. Its stated goal is to conquer the world and kill all who resist, and bring the whole world under sharia law. The fourth beast is the revived Islamic empire. Since it is reasonable, it passes the coherence test.

As I said before, it does not bring me joy to challenge the majority of scholars. However, I have a commitment to truth and could not have peace with myself if I did not share this new light on an old subject. For years I have been unable to reconcile what was happening in the world with what I had been taught and what I had read concerning the Last Days.

People kept asking me how Islam fits into the Last Day's scenario. This created in me a thirst to find out. As a result of my latest research, my mind is at ease that what I am presenting in this book is truth. It passes the truth test: correspondence and coherence.

CHAPTER TWELVE
DAY OF THE LORD

The phrase "day of the Lord" usually identifies events that take place at the end of history. It is often closely associated with the phrase "that day." One key to understanding these phrases is to note that they always identify a span of time during which God personally intervenes in history, directly or indirectly, to accomplish some specific aspect of His plan.

Most people associate the day of the Lord with a period of time or a special day that will occur when God's will and purpose for His world and for mankind will be fulfilled. Some scholars believe that the day of the Lord will be a longer period of time than a single day – a period of time when Christ will reign throughout the world before He cleanses heaven and earth in preparation for the eternal state of all mankind.

Other scholars believe the day of the Lord will be an instantaneous event when Christ returns to earth to redeem His faithful believers and send unbelievers to eternal damnation. There are sixteen mentions of the day of the Lord in the Old Testament and four mentions in the New Testament.[1]

From these general statements about the day of the Lord we surmise that there is a great deal of confusion and many different interpretations on the subject. I keep baring my soul in this book. For many, many years I have read the prophecies in Joel, Zephaniah, Ezekiel, Isaiah, Jeremiah, Zechariah, etc., and really could not connect all these prophecies in my mind. I could not understand why so much attention was given to these prophecies. For the most part, I thought of them as Israel fighting the surrounding countries which continued to attack her. Little thought was given to the possibility that these prophecies tell of Christ's war against the armies of the Mahdi Muslim Antichrist.

CHRIST'S WAR WITH MUSLIM NATIONS

We will start with a premise: Many of the prophecies concerning Israel's struggles refer to Christ and his army saving Israel from her enemies in the last great battle. The period associated with this battle is the day of the Lord. Again, I ask the reader to be patient as I give what I believe to be the literal, true interpretation of these prophecies.

We believe the Bible is inspired and every word is important. Our task is to make sure we are getting the true picture from what we read. Coming to what I believe is a scriptural interpretation of these prophecies has given me a sense of exhilaration, comfort, and assurance. Our part in the End Time's scenario is going to be an exciting adventure, to say the least.

JEHOVAH (CHRIST) FIGHTS ISRAEL'S ENEMIES

The first prophecy in the Bible dealing with Christ's attacking and destroying an Islamic country is Numbers 24:17-19.

> *I shall see him, but not now: I shall behold him, but not nigh: there shall come a Star out of Jacob, and a Sceptre shall rise out of Israel, and shall smite the corners of* **Moab**, *and destroy all the children of Sheth. And* **Edom** *shall be a possession,* **Seir** *also shall be a possession for his enemies; and Israel shall do valiantly. Out of Jacob shall come he that shall have dominion, and shall destroy him that remaineth of the city.*

Balam made this prophecy supposedly to curse Israel, but God turned the curse into a prophecy that Christ (the Star out of Jacob who is ruler) would destroy Moab. The three countries mentioned —Moab, Edom and Seir—refer to the people living east and southeast of Israel. Today this is definite Islamic territory. This prophecy has not been fulfilled as yet. But count on it: one day it will be fulfilled literally.

Ezekiel 35:1-6 speaks of this same prophecy.

> *Moreover the word of the LORD came unto me, saying, Son of man, set thy face against mount **Seir**, and prophesy against it, And say unto it, Thus saith the Lord GOD; Behold, O mount Seir, I am against thee, and I will stretch out mine hand against thee, and I will make thee most desolate. I will lay thy cities waste, and thou shalt be desolate, and thou shalt know that I am the LORD. Because thou hast had a perpetual hatred, and hast shed the blood of the children of Israel by the force of the sword in the time of their calamity, in the time that their iniquity had an end: Therefore, as I live, saith the Lord GOD, I will prepare thee unto blood, and blood shall pursue thee: since thou hast not hated blood, even blood shall pursue thee.*

JEHOVAH ON EARTH IS JESUS CHRIST

These prophecies describe Jehovah fighting, slaughtering His enemies. This, of course, is the resurrected, glorified Son of God. Isaiah 63:1-4 is an example.

> *Who is this that cometh from **Edom**, with dyed garments from Bozrah? this that is glorious in his apparel, travelling in the greatness of his strength? I that speak in righteousness, mighty to save. Wherefore art thou red in thine apparel, and thy garments like him that treadeth in the winefat?*

> *I have trodden the winepress alone; and of the people there was none with me: for I will tread them in mine anger, and trample them in my fury; and their blood shall be sprinkled upon my garments, and I will stain all my raiment. For the day of vengeance is in mine heart, and the year of my redeemed is come.*

This passage corresponds with Revelation 19:13-16,

> *And he was clothed with a vesture dipped in blood: and his name is called The Word of God… And out of his mouth goeth a sharp sword, that with it he should smite the nations: and he shall rule them with a rod of iron: and he treadeth the winepress of the fierceness and wrath of Almighty God. And he hath on his vesture and on his thigh a name written, KING OF KINGS, AND LORD OF LORDS.*

The Lord will judge Edom and all these Muslim lands for their perpetual and intense hatred of Israel. This enmity began after Mohammed established himself as undisputed leader of Medina. The Constitution of Medina was ratified by Mohammed with the Jews and pagans living in Medina, binding all parties to peaceful coexistence. Mohammed abrogated the treaty and declared war on the Jews.

Muslim historians Maxine Rodison and Ibn Warrick, as well as many others, record the atrocities Mohammed committed against the Jews. These sources describe Mohammed himself presiding over the beheading of at least 500 Jewish men. They were buried in a long ditch they dug for themselves. Their wives and daughters were sold for sex slaves and boys for labor.[2]

From that time to this. the hatred for Jews by Muslims has only intensified. God does not forget such cruelties to His chosen people. Ezekiel 25:6, *"For thus saith the Lord GOD; Because thou hast clapped thine hands, and stamped with the feet, and rejoiced in heart with all thy despite against the land of Israel.*

Ezekiel 25:13-14 speaks of Edom, Teman and Dedan. Teman is Yemen while Dedan is an ancient city in Saudi Arabia, now known as Al-Ula. Because of the use of both Teman and Dedan, we are to understand that the entire land mass stretching southward along the Red Sea and well into central Saudi Arabia is being highlighted. This is a massive area.[3]

> *Therefore thus saith the Lord GOD; I will also stretch out mine hand upon Edom, and will cut off man and beast from it; and I will make it desolate from Teman; and they of **Dedan** shall fall by the sword. And I will lay my vengeance upon Edom by the hand of my people Israel: and they shall do in Edom according to mine anger and according to my fury; and they shall know my vengeance, saith the Lord GOD.*

MESSIAH IN PERSON DEFEATS EGYPT AND LEBANON

Isaiah has many passages dealing with Jehovah (Jesus) judging and punishing Muslim nations. Let me share a couple that speak of Jehovah personally dealing with these nations. Isaiah 19:1-2,

> *The burden of Egypt. Behold, the LORD rideth upon a swift cloud, and shall come into Egypt: and the idols of Egypt shall be moved at his presence, and the heart of Egypt shall melt in the midst of it. And I will set the Egyptians against the Egyptians: and they shall fight every one against his brother, and every one against his neighbour; city against city, and kingdom against kingdom.*

Isaiah 10:33 speaks of Jehovah punishing Lebanon.

> *Behold, the Lord, the LORD of hosts, shall lop the bough with*

terror: and the high ones of stature shall be hewn down, and the haughty shall be humbled. And he shall cut down the thickets of the forest with iron, and Lebanon shall fall by a mighty one.

We could go on and on giving examples of Jehovah's wrath against all the Muslim nations surrounding Israel because of their hatred of Israel and blasphemy against God and His son, the Lord Jesus Christ. These prophecies emphasize the truth that God will certainly judge wickedness and will save His people from destruction.

DAY OF THE LORD ACCORDING TO JOEL

Joel chapter one describes the results of a locust invasion and the subsequent devastation of the land. Joel chapter two warns of the approach of the day of the Lord and proceeds to describe the battle and its combatants. I would suggest that you carefully read Joel chapter 2 right now. An army such as has never been is approaching says verse 2. It is important that we identify this army. This is not the army of the enemy but is Jehovah's army. By comparing Psalm 50, Isaiah 13, Daniel 7, Zechariah 14, Matthew 24:31 and Joel 2 we will see that both war and the rapture of the saints are evident in all six passages. At the end of the Tribulation, the martyred believers will be caught up and will join the previously raptured saints to accompany Christ as His warriors.

Psalm 50:3-5 speaks of God gathering His saints. What is this if not the rapture?

Our God shall come, and shall not keep silence: a fire shall devour before him, and it shall be very tempestuous round about him. He shall call to the heavens from above, and to the earth, that he may judge his people. **Gather my saints**

***together unto me**; those that have made a covenant with me by sacrifice.*

Matthew 24:31 speaks of the same gathering. *"And he shall send his angels with a great sound of a trumpet, and they shall **gather together his elect** from the four winds, from one end of heaven to the other."*

Zechariah 14:5 tells us that the saints are present in the battle.

*And ye shall flee to the valley of the mountains; for the valley of the mountains shall reach unto Azal: yea, ye shall flee, like as ye fled from before the earthquake in the days of Uzziah king of Judah: and the LORD my God shall come, and **all the saints with thee.***

The context is clear from Zechariah 14:3-4,

Then shall the LORD go forth, and fight against those nations, as when he fought in the day of battle. And his feet shall stand in that day upon the mount of Olives, which is before Jerusalem on the east, and the mount of Olives shall cleave in the midst thereof toward the east and toward the west, and there shall be a very great valley; and half of the mountain shall remove toward the north, and half of it toward the south.

Joel 2:16 speaks of the Bridegroom (Christ) and the bride (the raptured church). *"Gather the people, sanctify the congregation, assemble the elders, gather the children, and those that suck the breasts: let the **bridegroom** go forth of his chamber, and the **bride** out of her closet."* More examples could be given to show that the raptured saints will be in the battle with Christ. I believe the above is sufficient to honest readers.

SOLDIERS WITH GLORIFIED BODIES

Soldiers with glorified bodies cannot die! Read what Joel 2:8-10 says about these combatants in this war.

*Neither shall one thrust another; they shall walk every one in his path: and when they **fall upon the sword, they shall not be wounded**. They shall run to and fro in the city; they shall run upon the wall, they shall climb up upon the houses; they shall enter in at the windows like a thief. The earth shall quake before them; the heavens shall tremble: the sun and the moon shall be dark, and the stars shall withdraw their shining.*

The context is speaking of the miraculous—they run on the walls. How can people run on walls? With glorified bodies we can not only walk on walls but walk through them. In verse 11 we learn that this is the Lord's army. Joel 2:11, *"And the LORD shall utter his voice before **his army:** for his camp is very great: for he is strong that executeth his word: for the day of the LORD is great and very terrible; and who can abide it?"*

From the verses we have quoted it should be evident that, during the day of the Lord, Messiah speaks to His army in preparation for this battle for Jerusalem and is present with them.

SHARP SWORD COMING OUT OF HIS MOUTH

Revelation 19:15 needs some explanation. *"And out of his mouth goeth a sharp sword, that with it he should smite the nations: and he shall rule them with a rod of iron: and he treadeth the winepress of the fierceness and wrath of Almighty God."* Walid Shoebat interprets this differently than I have always believed. Comparing scripture with scripture, it seems that he is correct. This is how he explains this verse.

> This 'sharp sword' coming out of His mouth is the proclamation of war as written in Joel 2:11: *'And the LORD shall **utter his voice before his army:** for his camp is very great: for he is strong that executeth his word: for the day of the LORD is great and very terrible; and who can abide it?'* Some people claim that that this 'sword' is simply God destroying the enemies miraculously. Yet, the utterance from Messiah's mouth is a command. It is a command, an order, and a proclamation… Yet most Christians believe that a sword will come out of His mouth and poof! The enemy will be gone. Not so. The blade protruding from His mouth is symbolic, representing the Messiah's judgment upon the nations.
>
> In other words, Messiah will let Christians have a go at it. And indeed we will. This will indeed be the day when Christians participate in executing justice… The false bravery of Muslim warriors, the wolf packs that rape and kill innocent Christian women in Armenia, Sudan, and Lebanon will see the day when these women come back at them and their cowardly faces are wrenched with pain: Joel 2:6, *'Before their face the people shall be much pained: all faces shall gather blackness.'*…
>
> That's right, you cowards that kill yourselves and others. Kim-Sun-Il, the Korean translator that you killed is coming back. As the Messiah returns, so will he. This time it is you who will beg for your life while your teeth gnash with trembling and fear. What goes around will come around. **God is just!**[4]

Revelation 6:9 fits here.

> *And when he had opened the fifth seal, I saw under the altar the souls of them that were slain for the word of God, and for the testimony which they held: And they cried with a loud voice, saying, How long, O Lord, holy and true, dost thou not judge and avenge our blood on them that dwell on the earth? And white robes were given unto every one of them; and it was said unto them, that they should rest yet for a little season, **until** their fellowservants also and their brethren, that should be killed as they were, should be fulfilled.*

Their prayer will be answered as in Revelation 19:14, *"And the armies which were in heaven followed him upon white horses, clothed in fine linen, white and clean."* At last, these persecuted saints would have vindication against those who so cruelly beheaded them.

JUDGMENT OF THE NATIONS

There is a definite connection between Matthew 25 and Joel 3; both refer to the same event. Matthew 25:32-41 speaks of the judgment of the nations. The key to the correct interpretation of this passage is to identify who are "my brethren." Some argue that "my brethren" are the Church; others say Israel. Without a doubt "my brethren" refers to Israel. The whole context and the gathering of the nations all have to do with Israel.

> *And before him shall be gathered all nations: and he shall separate them one from another, as a shepherd divideth his sheep from the goats: And he shall set the sheep on his right hand, but the goats on the left. Then shall the King say unto them on his right hand, Come, ye blessed of my Father, inherit the kingdom prepared for you from the foundation of*

*the world: For I was an hungred, and ye gave me meat: I was thirsty, and ye gave me drink: I was a stranger, and ye took me in: Naked, and ye clothed me: I was sick, and ye visited me: I was in prison, and ye came unto me. Then shall the righteous answer him, saying, Lord, when saw we thee an hungred, and fed thee? or thirsty, and gave thee drink? When saw we thee a stranger, and took thee in? or naked, and clothed thee? Or when saw we thee sick, or in prison, and came unto thee? And the King shall answer and say unto them, Verily I say unto you, Inasmuch as ye have done it unto one of the least of these **my brethren**, ye have done it unto me. Then shall he say also unto them on the left hand, Depart from me, ye cursed, into everlasting fire, prepared for the devil and his angels.*

The nations will be judged as to how they related to Israel during the difficult Tribulation Period. Joel 3:2 speaks of this same event.

I will also gather all nations, and will bring them down into the valley of Jehoshaphat, and will plead with them there for my people and for my heritage Israel, whom they have scattered among the nations, and parted my land.

Joel 3:11-12 shows us the same judgment of the nations.

Assemble yourselves, and come, all ye heathen, and gather yourselves together round about: thither cause thy mighty ones to come down, O LORD. Let the heathen be wakened, and come up to the valley of Jehoshaphat: for there will I sit to judge all the heathen round about.

History teaches us that God has blessed those nations that have been kind to Israel, for example, England and the United States. Think how God blessed that little island of Great Britain and made her ruler of half the nations of the globe so that the sun never set on the British Empire. Note how Great Britain championed the cause of Israel. The **Balfour Declaration of 1917** (dated 2 November 1917) was a formal statement of policy by the British government stating:

> His Majesty's government view with favour the establishment in Palestine of a national home for the Jewish people, and will use their best endeavors to facilitate the achievement of this object, it being clearly understood that nothing shall be done which may prejudice the civil and religious rights of existing non-Jewish communities in Palestine, or the rights and political status enjoyed by Jews in any other country.[5]

God was mindful of this kindness and rewarded them richly.

It was no other than President Harry Truman in 1948 who opened the way for the United Nations to declare Israel a sovereign nation.[6] Oh, how God has blessed America and made her the land of the free and home of the brave! The American experience of freedom is a new, wonderful thing in the history of mankind: free to pursue life, liberty, and happiness. I believe God has blessed America for two reasons: first, their goodness to Jews living in America and for standing with the nation Israel against her enemies; and second, because American churches send missionaries and money to spread the Gospel around the world.

On the other hand, He has judged those nations that have tried to exterminate Jews, for example, Hitler's Germany and Stalin's Russia.

Islam is rising and will rise. That ascendancy will be temporary in the will and plan of God. Islamic nations along with their Mahdi and False Jesus will be cast into the pit. The nations of the Tribulation Period will be judged as to how they treated "my brethren" i.e., the Jewish people during the terrible days of the Tribulation.

CHAPTER THIRTEEN
THE HARLOT, MYSTERY BABYLON, AND THE BEAST

Our intent in this chapter is to identify the Harlot, Mystery Babylon, and the Beast that the Harlot rides. Revelation 17:3 says, "*So he carried me (the Apostle John) away in the spirit into the wilderness* (literally, a desert): *and I saw a woman sit upon a scarlet coloured beast, full of names of blasphemy, having seven heads and ten horns.*"

THE HARLOT (PROSTITUTE)

The great majority of prophecy teachers hold that the Harlot is the apostate Christian church, i.e., Protestant, Orthodox, and Roman Catholic. Dr. Zomaya Solomon, author of the *The Beast and the End-Times Events,* sums it up well. "While the term, "woman," here speaks of the end-time Apostate Church in its entirety—Protestant, Orthodox, and Catholic—the ecumenical church could well also be led by a woman."[1] Some have suggested the Harlot city to be Rome or New York. Another view holds that the Harlot stands for "the combination universal religion" and is political in nature. However, neither Rome, New York nor the combination universal religion conform to the basic scriptural description of the Harlot. To accurately identify the Harlot we must look at all the Biblical data.

LOCATION OF THE HARLOT CITY

Isaiah 21 refers to the fall of Babylon and locates it in "the desert of the sea." The well-known Middle East historian, Bernard Lewis, identifies the desert of the sea to be Arabia.[2] Verse 9 says, *"And, behold, here cometh a chariot of men, with a couple of horsemen. And he answered and said, Babylon is fallen, is fallen; and all the graven images of her gods he hath broken unto the ground."* The exact same announcement is made in Revelation 18:1, 2.

And after these things I saw another angel come down from heaven, having great power; and the earth was lightened with his glory. And he cried mightily with a strong voice, saying, Babylon the great is fallen, is fallen, and is become the habitation of devils, and the hold of every foul spirit, and a cage of every unclean and hateful bird.

Notice how this corresponds with *"So he carried me (the Apostle John) away in the spirit into the wilderness* (literally, a desert): *and I saw a woman sit upon a scarlet coloured beast, full of names of blasphemy, having seven heads and ten horns."* (Revelation 17:3). All of the locations mentioned in Isaiah 21 are in Arabia: Dumah, v. 11, Arabia, v. 13, Kedar, v. 16. Walid Shoebat gives the possible locations of the Harlot city and the Mystery Babylon as follows:

There are many conjectures concerning Mystery Babylon. Some say that Babylon is the United States of America or the Vatican. However, none of these theories are supported by the text. Either students of the Bible build a mold from Scripture or they make the Scriptures fit their theories. There are really only these two choices. Once we read the text of Isaiah 21, it becomes quite clear: "An oracle concerning the Desert of the Sea" (Isaiah 21:1) This is not the Tigris and Euphrates rivers in Iraq, but on a literal sea surrounded by the mass of waters in the Persian-Arab Sea, Indian Ocean, and Red Sea. It is also thought that "the sea" may be a reference to the Nufud desert, a virtual ocean of enormous sand dunes. The camel was called the ship of the desert sea, the only formidable vehicle to transport through desert sand.[3]

CHARACTERISTICS OF THE HARLOT

As we discuss the Harlot and the Beast we need to clarify to what we are referring. The Beast is a coalition of ten kings representing the seven kingdoms of the past, under the authority of the Antichrist. The Harlot is a separate distinct geographical entity that represents the religious source of Antichrist's religion. Very specifically Revelation 17:18 tell us "*the woman (the Harlot) is the great city that rules over the kings of the earth.*"

Revelation 17:1-6,18 gives much information about the harlot.

And there came one of the seven angels which had the seven vials, and talked with me, saying unto me, Come hither; I will shew unto thee the judgment of the great whore that sitteth upon many waters: With whom the kings of the earth have committed fornication, and the inhabitants of the earth have been made drunk with the wine of her fornication. So he carried me away in the spirit into the wilderness: and I saw a woman sit upon a scarlet coloured beast, full of names of blasphemy, having seven heads and ten horns. And the woman was arrayed in purple and scarlet colour, and decked with gold and precious stones and pearls, having a golden cup in her hand full of abominations and filthiness of her fornication: And upon her forehead was a name written, MYSTERY, BABYLON THE GREAT, THE MOTHER OF HARLOTS AND ABOMINATIONS OF THE EARTH. And I saw the woman drunken with the blood of the saints, and with the blood of the martyrs of Jesus: and when I saw her, I wondered with great admiration…And the woman which thou sawest *is that **great city**, which reigneth over the kings of the earth.*

Let us carefully glean the facts revealed to us from this passage. First, the whore or the Harlot sits upon many waters. The angel takes John into the desert to see this Harlot city that "sits upon many waters." Verse 15 tells us what this means: *"And he saith unto me, The waters which thou sawest, where the whore sitteth, are peoples, and multitudes, and nations, and tongues."* This indicates that the Harlot city exerts strong spiritual influence over a great mixture of different ethnicities and languages. Can you think of any city that has influenced more nationalities than Mecca? Every faithful Muslim is duty bound to visit Mecca and go through prescribed rituals.

Second, we learn that *"the kings of the earth have committed fornication, and the inhabitants of the earth have been made drunk with the wine of her fornication"* (Revelation 17:2). Another important question is what kind of wine does a desert produce? Certainly not wine made of grapes! Most prophecy teachers hold that the wine here represents the wine and the chalice of the Catholic Church's communion. However, the wine allegorically speaks of oil! What desert wine intoxicates the earth and causes this desert region to grow filthy rich? This will be a new thought for many. Think it through. The Harlot uses both Islam and oil as her "wine" through which she seduces the nations of the world into spiritual adultery. Since 1973 Saudi Arabia has spent 78 billion dollars to spread Islam to the West.[4] Oil will also be the lure for turning nations against Israel, the Harlot's great enemy.

Isaiah 34:8-10 and context speak of God's judgment upon the nations that persecuted Israel and verse 6 specially mentions Idumea and Bozra (Muslim countries).

> *For it is the day of the LORD'S vengeance, and the year of recompences for the controversy of Zion. And **the streams thereof shall be turned into pitch,** and the dust thereof into brimstone, and the land thereof shall become burning pitch.*

> *It shall not be quenched night nor day; the smoke thereof shall go up for ever: from generation to generation it shall lie waste; none shall pass through it for ever and ever.*

Undoubtedly, this "pitch" speaks of the crude oil so plentiful in these Muslims lands.

Third, the Harlot is dressed in a scarlet robe decked with jewels, pearls, and gold. *"And the woman was arrayed in purple and scarlet colour, and decked with gold and precious stones and pearls, having a golden cup in her hand full of abominations and filthiness of her fornication."* Scarlet or crimson speaks of royalty. It also is identified with sinfulness (Isaiah 1:18). Royalty, riches, and sinfulness characterize the Harlot. What Islamic desert country is governed by a royal monarchy that is filthy rich and utterly corrupt? Saudi Arabia fits.

Fourth, the Harlot was "drunk with the blood of the saints." Both the Beast and the Harlot behead the saints. In a previous chapter we learned how decapitation has been used by Muslims in days gone by, is presently, and will be more so in the future during the Great Tribulation.

Fifth, the Harlot is a city. Revelation 17:18 makes this clear: *And the woman which thou sawest is that **great city**, which reigneth over the kings of the earth."* This city rules over the kings of the earth signifying that it is a political and geographical entity. What city in the earth has usurped the privilege of being the spiritual capitol of the world? Toward what city do over a billion Muslims bow five times a day to pray?

Much more could be written about the Harlot of Revelation 17. To crystallize our thoughts let us review what we have learned. The harlot city is located in the 'desert of the sea' which is Arabia. The Harlot 'sits upon many waters' which are peoples, and multitudes, and tongues. The influence of Mecca reaches round the globe.

The Harlot's wine (oil) intoxicates the nations of the world. The nations are addicted to the wine or oil of which the Harlot has abundance.

The Harlot is dressed in a scarlet robe decked with precious jewels and gold. The scarlet robe speaks of royalty and wickedness and the jewels and gold speak of unbelievable wealth.

The Harlot is a great city. Annually, millions of Muslims travel to Mecca. The trip is called the *Hajj*. Those that make this trip are called *Hajjis*.

Daily, multiplied millions turn toward Mecca and pray to their god, Allah.

DESTRUCTION OF THE HARLOT

Revelation 17:16-18 tell us that the Beast hates the Harlot and will finally turn on her, kill her, and burn her with fire.

> *And the ten horns which thou sawest upon the beast, these shall hate the whore, and shall make her desolate and naked, and shall eat her flesh, and burn her with fire. For God hath put in their hearts to fulfil his will, and to agree, and give their kingdom unto the beast, until the words of God shall be fulfilled. And the woman which thou sawest is that great city, which reigneth over the kings of the earth.*

Some find it hard to believe that Muslims would destroy their most holy city with the Kabla (Islam's most holy shrine) and the small black stone (an object of worship kept in the Kabla). Those who take the Western view of Mystery Babylon being Rome or New York could be asked the same question, i.e., how could Europe burn Rome?

The possibility of Muslims destroying Mecca and Saudi Arabia is not beyond the pale of possibility. In the Seventh Century Muslim armies laid seige to Mecca and destroyed much of the Kabla with stones from catapults. During the First World War Ottoman

Turks attacked Saudi Arabia causing the Arabs to ally with the British to defeat the Turks. More recently, on November 20, 1979, over 500 militants attacked the holy city (Mecca). In July 1987, over 400 people died as a result of Ayatollah Khomeini disrupting the annual Hajj.[5] During the Gulf War, Saddam Hussain sent numerous scud missiles over Saudi Arabia. The Turks have no love for the Arabs and resent the Arab imperialism promoted by Saudi Arabia. So, the possibility of an attack on Mecca and Saudi Arabia by the Beast (Muslim Coalition) is not far-fetched at all.

DESTRUCTION OF MECCA AND MEDINA PREDICTED IN ISLAMIC PROPHECY

The fact that the Antichrist, the Muslim Mahdi, will attack and destroy these cities is found in Muslim traditions:

The final battle will be waged by Muslim faithful coming on the backs of horses…carrying black banners. They will stand on the side of the Jordan River and will wage war that the earth has never seen before. The true Messiah who is the Islamic Mahdi…will defeat Europe…will lead this army of Seljuks (Turks), He will preside over the world from Jerusalem because **Mecca** *would have been* **destroyed**.[6]

Another tradition says this:

The flourishing state of Jerusalem will be when Yathrib (Medina) is in ruins, the ruined state of Yathrib will be when the Great War comes, the outbreak of the Great War at the conquest of Constantinople and the conquest of Constantinople when the Dajjal (the Antichrist) comes forth.[7]

Radical Islam does not discriminate. It happily kills its own as well as infidels. The Islamic coalition established by the Mahdi will destroy Saudi Arabia. Seeing this prophecy of theirs fulfilled will embolden them to believe they are indeed acting according to Allah's plan.

GOD WARNING TO FLEE

Revelation 18:1-4 warn God's people living in Babylon to flee.

And after these things I saw another angel come down from heaven, having great power; and the earth was lightened with his glory. And he cried mightily with a strong voice, saying, Babylon the great is fallen, is fallen, and is become the habitation of devils, and the hold of every foul spirit, and a cage of every unclean and hateful bird. For all nations have drunk of the wine of the wrath of her fornication, and the kings of the earth have committed fornication with her, and the merchants of the earth are waxed rich through the abundance of her delicacies. And I heard another voice from heaven, saying, Come out of her, my people, that ye be not partakers of her sins, and that ye receive not of her plagues.

This was prophesied by the Prophet Jeremiah in chapters 50 and 51. Jeremiah 51:6,9 says,

*Flee out of the midst of Babylon, and deliver every man his soul: be not cut off in her iniquity; for this is the time of the LORD'S vengeance; he will render unto her a recompence… Babylon hath been a golden cup in the LORD'S hand, that made all the earth drunken: the nations have drunken of her wine; therefore the nations are mad… We would have healed Babylon, but she is not healed: forsake her, and let us go every **one into his own country**: for her judgment reacheth unto* *heaven, and is lifted up even to the skies.*

People are warned to flee everyone to his own country. Like the ancient Babylon, so also is the Last-Day's Babylon or Mystery Babylon filled with expatriates and foreigners. In fact, there are 18 million citizens and six million foreign workers in Saudi Arabia today.[8] What Arab, Islamic, desert nation is filled with a massive laborforce who are only used for labor and are never offered citizenship? You guessed it. Saudi Arabia!

MYSTERY BABYLON

Babylon is mentioned six times in the book of Revelation and Mystery Babylon is mentioned only once. Revelation 17:5 says,

And upon her forehead was a name written, MYSTERY, BABYLON THE GREAT, THE MOTHER OF HARLOTS AND ABOMINATIONS OF THE EARTH. And I saw the woman drunken with the blood of the saints, and with the blood of the martyrs of Jesus: and when I saw her, I wondered with great admiration.

From these verses we learn that the Harlot is the city of Last Day's Babylon referred to as Mystery Babylon. Revelation 17:18 makes this clear. *"And the woman which thou sawest is that great city, which reigneth over the kings of the earth."*

Walid Shoebat, a converted Muslim explains the term "mother of all harlots" like this:

It does not mean that she was the source of all forms of idolatry. This is an "eastern" expression expressing the superlative degree. We remember Saddam Hussain vainly boasting that the battle for Baghdad would be the "mother of all battles." He also said America would suffer the "mother of all defeats." Mystery Babylon, the Harlot city, Mecca, the womb of Islam, is the greatest manifestation of spiritual infidelity against the God of the Bible that has ever existed throughout the history of the world. Throughout history, many "prostitutes" or false religions exist and have existed, but the Great Harlot is portrayed here as being by far the most significant of them all. The Harlot's false religion is also a mystery in that like no other pagan religion, it sprouts from a mixture of a heretical Christian cult and a pagan Moon-god religion that has attempted to cloak itself with certain Jewish and Christian elements in order to appear as a biblical faith and the rightful successor of the Judeo-Christian tradition. When the veil is pulled back, Islam's true nature and pagan source become apparent. It is a religion that denies the essence of God, contradicts His character and blasphemes His attributes.[9]

THE BEAST

The book of Revelation and the book of Daniel teach concerning the Beast. In Daniel 2, Daniel interprets the King's dream, revealing that it represented four world empires. Then in Daniel 7 Daniel has a dream which is very similar to Nebuchadnezzar's. He tells us that four beasts came up from the sea (humanity). The beasts are said to be empires rising from the sea. The lion, Babylon; the bear, Medo-Persia; and the leopard, Greece and Rome are followed by the fourth beast, the Islamic empire, which is described as *dreadful, terrible, and strong exceedingly, with great iron teeth it devoured and brake in pieces and stamped the residue with its feet.* So, first we learn that the Beast is an empire.

Daniel 7:17 adds another dimension. *"These great beasts, which are four, are four kings, which shall arise out of the earth."* The fourth king is the Antichrist who kills the saints until the Ancient of days crushes him and gives the kingdom to the saints.

BEAST OF REVELATION

The first mention of the Beast in Revelation portrays him contending with the Two Witnesses, killing them and making war against the saints (Revelation 11:7). Next, in Revelation 13:1, the Beast rises up out of the sea. Verse 2 is very important to our premise that the fourth Kingdom is Islam and the Beast is the Muslim Mahdi. *"And the beast which I saw was like unto a leopard, and his feet were as the feet of a bear, and his mouth as the mouth of a lion: and the dragon gave him his power, and his seat, and great authority."* The fourth Beast and the fourth kingdom must be a composite of the three kingdoms that went before. The Islamic Empire is a composite of Babylon, Persia, and Greece. The Roman Empire is not as it never conquered these territories.

In verses 11 and 12 another Beast appears.

> *I beheld another beast coming up out of the earth; and he had two horns like a lamb, and he spake as a dragon. And he exerciseth all the power of the first beast before him, and causeth the earth and them which dwell therein to worship the first beast, whose deadly wound was healed.*

This, of course, is the False Prophet who heads up the religious affairs of Antichrist's empire. He forces worship of the Beast by requiring the mark of the beast, without which no man can buy or sell. Interestingly, those who are martyred for not receiving the mark of the beast are said to be victors instead of victims. Revelation 15:2 says,

> *And I saw as it were a sea of glass mingled with fire: and them*

*that had gotten the **victory** over the beast, and over his image, and over his mark, and over the number of his name, stand on the sea of glass, having the harps of God.*

Those who compromised, rationalized or whatever, and received the mark of the beast suffer the consequences. Revelation 16:2 tells about it. *"And the first went, and poured out his vial upon the earth; and there fell a noisome and grievous sore upon the men which had the mark of the beast, and upon them which worshipped his image."*

BEAST'S RELATIONSHIP WITH THE HARLOT

Remember that the Harlot is a city and the Beast is a kingdom, the kingdom of Antichrist. Thus, the Harlot and the Beast are two separate entities but with a close relationship. We see the nature of this relationship in Revelation 17:7, *"And the angel said unto me, Wherefore didst thou marvel? I will tell thee the mystery of the woman, and of the **beast that carrieth her,** which hath the seven heads and ten horns."* The Beast is the governmental aspect of the Antichrist Empire, and the Harlot city is the spiritual driver of this Beast mechanism. For a time the Harlot and the Beast harmoniously pursued their ambitions and pleasures. Things do change. Revelation 17:16 says, *"And the ten horns (the Muslim coalition) which thou sawest upon the beast, these shall hate the whore, and shall make her desolate and naked, and shall eat her flesh, and burn her with fire."*

DEMISE OF THE BEAST

The Beast and his armies gather to fight Christ and His army. Revelation 19:19 describe it. *"And I saw the beast, and the kings of the earth, and their armies, gathered together to make war against him that sat on the horse, and against his army."* Predictably, the Beast and his army were no match for Christ and His army. Verses 20,21 give the results.

> *And the beast was taken, and with him the false prophet that wrought miracles before him, with which he deceived them that had received the mark of the beast, and them that worshipped his image. These both were cast alive into a lake of fire burning with brimstone. And the remnant (the ten kings and their armies) were slain with the sword of him that sat upon the horse, which sword proceeded out of his mouth: and all the fowls were filled with their flesh.*

CONCLUSION

More so much more could be written. The title of this book, *Islam and the End Times*, probably has many of you in shock by now. I, too, was in a state of shock as I studied and researched this matter. I hasten to say that I now have peace that I am seeking to be a good "Berean" by testing everything with the Word of God. Molding my interpretations to conform to traditional views is not my modus operandi. I seek truth wherever it leads.

POSSIBLE OBJECTIONS

The first objection to surface concerns the seven hills on which the woman sits. Revelation 17:9 says, *"And here is the mind which hath wisdom. The seven heads are seven mountains, on which the woman sitteth."* Since Rome is said to be built upon seven hills, many interpreters conclude that the place on which the woman sits must be Rome. Ancient Babylon was said to be built upon seven artificial hills. Constantinople, called the second Rome is also built on seven hills. The context shows that these "mountains" better than hills are not literal but represent seven kingdoms. The seven heads mentioned in the verse are certainly seven kings.

The second objection has to do with the Greek word *eremon* which translates wilderness or desert. Revelation 17:3 says John was carried away by an angel into the *eremon* or desert. Objectors say the desert is not to be taken literally. They say the desert was just the "theatre" for John to see the vision. But why not take it literally? Let the word mean what it says. John was taken to a literal desert to see a city in the desert. Period. Mecca sits on a barren valley surrounded by mountains. This interpretation passes the coherence test. It is reasonable.

REASONS TO BELIEVE ARABIA, NOT ROME

Several European countries are mentioned including Rome. But there is no word concerning their destruction. However, Arabia and surrounding Muslim nations are named and doomed to destruction.

Arabia does have great influence over the kings of the earth by virtue of its oil, an intoxicating commodity to oil-starved countries. Rome has no such addictive substance.

Rome exports all the items mentioned in Revelation 18:11,12.

And the merchants of the earth shall weep and mourn over her; for no man buyeth their merchandise any more: The merchandise of gold, and silver, and precious stones, and of pearls, and fine linen, and purple, and silk, and scarlet, and all thyine wood, and all manner vessels of ivory, and all manner vessels of most precious wood, and of brass, and iron, and marble.

Yet the Harlot city, Mecca, produces none of theses things but imports them all. Mecca buys, imports while Rome sells and exports. The merchants are sad for they no longer are able to ship these luxuries to the destroyed city.

Arabia has a huge foreign workforce. Rome does not. Rome allows it foreign workers citizenship. Arabia does not. Arabia persecutes the saints, beheading them. Rome does not. Arabia is in a desert. Rome is not. Arabia imports slaves. Rome does not.

So we come back to the truth test. The premise that Mecca in the Saudi Arabian desert is the Harlot city passes the two tests of correspondence to the facts and being completely reasonable in light of current events.

CHAPTER FOURTEEN
REVIVED ISLAMIC EMPIRE - THE CALIPHATE

The word *caliphate (khalifa* in Arabic) comes from the word *caliph,* (*khalif* in Arabic) the temporal and spiritual ruler of Muslim countries. The caliph is essentially the vicar of Mohammed as the pope is the vicar of Christ to Roman Catholics. This is the only form of government that is fully sanctioned by Islamic jurisprudence. The first caliph was Abu Bakr who took leadership at the death of Mohammed. The leader of the Ottoman Empire was the last caliph. This empire ruled over Turkey, Egypt, modern day Iran, Iraq, Syria, Jordan, Bulgaria, Albania and all the Muslim countries in the former USSR. In 1924 the British and their allies abolished the Ottoman Empire because of its support of Kaiser Wilhelm and Germany in the First World War. After fourteen centuries this beast of an empire was slain. For eighty-six years Muslims have been without a caliph and without a caliphate.

ASPIRATION FOR A REVIVED CALIPHATE

Modern Islamism, as headed by the Muslim Brotherhood, Yusuf al-Qaradawi, Osama bin Laden and others, has contended that the reestablishment of the caliphate is the ultimate goal for its struggle against secularism and Western societies.[1] Muslim people who once viewed themselves as the world's superpower for thirteen hundred years have seen their empire disintegrate into a group of separate, backwater, underachieving states ruled by power-hungry dictators.

Muslims have a sense of entitlement believing that world

domination is their destiny. True Muslims have no doubt about the final outcome. However, their frustration mounts as they see the nations who embrace the Judaeo-Christian heritage (Europe and North America) prospering especially financially, technologically and militarily. Overall, the psychological impact and resentment of the Muslim world is all consuming. The once great thriving Muslim caliphate now is a shame to Muslims. In Eastern culture, nothing in their value system comes close to shame and honor. When things go awry then the first move is to blame someone or something for the trouble. Muslims blame all their ills on Israel or, as they call it, "The World Zionist Conspiracy," along with the crusader forces of Christian England and America.

Walid Shoebat, former Muslim terrorist, knows the Muslim mind and this is what he says about the coming caliphate:

> Looking back at pre-colonial days of Islamic Empire, two thoughts often emerge in the modern Muslim mind. The first is to recapture their former glory, and the second is to punish those who have withheld it for so long. All of these aspirations are most often summarized negatively in the overthrow and destruction of Israel and the West, while they are expressed positively in the messianic expectations concerning the re-establishment of the caliphate.[2]

PRO-CALIPHATE GROUPS ADVANCE

In February of 2006, Sheik Ismail Nawahda of Guiding Helper Foundation preached to a gathering on the Temple Mount in Jerusalem. He called on them to restore the caliphate as "Genuine Islamic Rule," which would unite all Muslims in the world against the infidels. A few months later, Sheik Raed Salah of the Islamic Movement declared to 50,000 Muslims outside of Haifa that,

Jerusalem will soon be capital of a Moslem Arab caliphate, and efforts by the Israeli establishment to Judaize the city will amount to nothing...soon Jerusalem will be the capital of the new Muslim caliphate, and the caliph's seat will be there.[3]

CALIPHATE A THREAT TO THE WEST

The main reason is because a caliphate will give legitimacy to jihad. The jihadists and the Islamists that fuel the terrorist movements today are radicals and are operating outside the *ummah* i.e., the Muslim community. But once a caliph is in office, it is actual law for him to engage the non-Muslim world in war in order to spread Islam.

Today jihad is comparable to guerilla warfare, i.e., spasmodic and temporary with few combatants. But once Muslims unite under a caliph there will be all-out-war. Not a bombing here and there, but the world's first full-scale religious war. It would involve everything the Muslim world could throw out, from economic jihad to withholding oil to cyber jihad to multi-front military conflicts.

Mark Gabriel, a converted Egyptian Muslim, teaches what true jihad is all about:

> The jihad stage commences when Muslims are a minority with strength, influence, and power. At this stage every Muslim's duty is to actively fight the enemy, overturning the system of the non-Muslim country and establishing Islamic authority. This stage is based on the final revelation (Mohammed) received concerning jihad. Surah 9:5 says, *"So when the sacred months have passed away, then slay the idolaters wherever you find them, and take them captives and besiege them and lie in wait for them in every ambush, then if they repent and keep up prayer and pay the poor-rate, leave*

their way free to them; surely Allah is Forgiving, Merciful." Muslims are commanded to kill everyone who chooses not to convert to Islam. The verse says "Wherever you find them." There is no geographical limit.[4]

True Muslims believe their book, and when commanded by their leaders to kill, then watch out!

TURKEY WILL BE HEADQUARTERS OF THE CALIPHATE

Ample evidence exists to prove that Turkey will be a main player in the move to restore the caliphate.

SCRIPTURAL EVIDENCES

First, the prominence of Turkey in Ezekiel 38 proves this fact. Five of the eight locations mentioned are within Turkey, i.e., Magog, Meshech, Tubal, Togormah and Gomer.

Second, Revelation 17 speaks of the seventh empire which has ten horns. The beast represents an empire with ten kingdoms. Verse 7 says *"And the angel said unto me, Wherefore didst thou marvel? I will tell thee the mystery of the woman, and of the beast that carrieth her,* **which hath the seven heads and ten horns."** Now verse 9 interprets for us what are the seven heads. *"And here is the mind which hath wisdom. The seven heads are seven mountains, on which the woman sitteth."* Mountains as we have seen represent kingdoms or empires. The seven heads are the following:

The Egyptian Empire
The Assyrian Empire
The Babylonian Empire
The Medo-Persian Empire

The Macedonian Greek Empire
The Roman Empire
The Islamic Empire

A comparison of Revelation 13:3 and 17:11 bring light on the subject of the seventh empire, the Islamic Empire. *"And I saw one of his heads as it were wounded to death; and his deadly wound was healed: and all the world wondered after the beast"* (13:3). Then 17:11 says, *"And the beast that was, and is not, even he is the eighth, and is of the seven, and goeth into perdition."* The "eighth" refers to the last empire, i.e., the revived Islamic Empire which will be destroyed in the battle of Armageddon. Please stay with me and we will understand the meaning of these verses.

The heads are empires according to verse 9. Previously, we saw that the Islamic Empire is the seventh empire or head. We also learned that the Ottoman Empire was abolished by the Allies after World War I. Verse 11 tells us, *"the beast that was,"* i.e., the Islamic Empire, was but now is not because it has been destroyed. Then we are told that he (the Beast, i.e., its head) Antichrist will go into perdition. Remember that the kingdom and the king are both referred to as the Beast.

Third, Daniel 11 foretell the history of the Seleucid or the Greek Empire. It tells of Alexander the Great and how his kingdom was divided into four kingdoms. The King of the North is Antiochus IV Epiphanies, who is a prefigure of the Antichrist. Daniel 11:31 speak of the ungodly acts of Antiochus which is a foreshadowing of what Antichrist will do. *"And they shall pollute the sanctuary of strength,*(Temple) *and shall take away the daily sacrifice, and they shall place the abomination that maketh desolate."* Since Antiochus came from the Seleucid Empire of which modern day Turkey was a part, then we can expect Antichrist to come from this very area.

Fourth, Zechariah 9 speaks of the final battle (Armageddon) before the Messiah Christ proclaims peace to the nations. Verses 13 and 14 speak of Judah and Ephraim fighting the Greeks.

> *When I have bent Judah for me, filled the bow with Ephraim, and raised up thy sons, O Zion, against thy sons, O **Greece**, and made thee as the sword of a mighty man. And the LORD shall be seen over them, and his arrow shall go forth as the lightning: and the Lord GOD shall blow the trumpet, and shall go with whirlwinds of the south.*

A better translation for Greece would be **Javan**. Javan was a descendant of Noah who came to live on the western coast of Asia Minor or modern-day Turkey.

TURKEY, MEDIATOR BETWEEN WEST AND EAST

A look at the map shows that Turkey is indeed the bridge between East and West, Europe and the Middle East, and Israel and the Muslim world. After the Second World War, Mustafa Kemal Ataturk, a political genius, created the modern political nation of Turkey. By means of numerous checks and balances a democratic, secular government has successfully ruled in spite of its Muslim population. Turkey has stood alone among hostile Muslim neighbors and has embraced significant secular and even Western values. Although changes are in the air, even now the governments of Israel and the United States rest securely in believing that Turkey is a trustworthy ally.[5]

Turkey will certainly be the key player in any negotiations between Israel, the European Union, the United States and any Muslim coalition. Professor Ruben Safrastyan of Acharyan University in Yerevan, Armenia says:

> The pro-Islamist party (JDP) in 2002 restructured...the basic directions of the Turkish foreign policy...The foreign

Minister of the country was instructed to improve relations with the Arab states and Iran, at the same time conserving allied relations with Israel on quite a cool level. As a result Turkey will have the opportunity to get a mediating role both in the Middle East conflict and in the controversial relations between some Middle-Eastern countries and the West. Therefore, Turkey will become a key state in the region, which will enhance its significance for the European Union and accelerate the process of Turkey's accession to that organization.[6]

This is very significant as we know that during the Tribulation Period there will be serious negotiations and treaties between Israel and the revived Islamic Empire. Turkey is planning on being the key negotiator.

TURKEY'S MOVE TOWARD ISLAMISM

World Magazine in November, 2009 published an article entitled, "Switching Sides." Pictured shaking hands are Turkish Prime minister Erdogan and President Ahmadinejad of Iran. The lead sentence tells the story:

A major shift has taken place in the geopolitics of the Middle East. Turkey, a strategic ally of the West and Israel — and the only Muslim country in the region with a secular government besides fractured Iraq — has effectively signaled that it's leaving its Western friends and reorienting itself eastward.[7]

The article goes on to reveal more about Turkey's future and its intent for moving away from the West.

Part of the reason [for Turkey's embrace of Syria] is that the

Turks have been carefully advancing the notion that Turkey may emerge as **a neo-Ottoman Empire caliphate**. The Ottoman Empire controlled much of the Arab world, including Syria...Turkey has already joined the Iranian axis: These events give a great push to the most destabilizing countries in the region—Iran and Syria. Similarly, the U.S. and NATO now need to deal with the fact that a linchpin state in the Western alliance has effectively switched teams.[8]

TURKEY'S MILITARY MIGHT

Antichrist will be a warrior. To be a military leader, needless to say, an army is essential. Few Americans are aware that Turkey has the second largest army in the world, second only to the United States. In fact, Turkey's army far supersedes the militaries of Germany, Spain, Italy and England combined.[9] Turkey has the military capital necessary to enforce any Middle East peace plan. This nation has the military capabilities to attack and defeat any number of surrounding nations in the area. Any coalition of Muslim nations joining Turkey would be formidable. It fits the description of the final empire of Daniel 7:19.

> *Then I would know the truth of the fourth beast, which was diverse from all the others, exceeding dreadful, whose teeth were of iron, and his nails of brass; which devoured, brake in pieces, and stamped the residue with his feet.*

TURKEY – ANTI-SEMITIC AND ANTI-CHRISTIAN

Turkey has a sad history of hatred for Christians and Jews. What most people do not know is that the Muslim Turks have slaughtered an estimated 2.8 million Christians. Stanley Cohen, professor of criminology at Hebrew University in Jerusalem writes:

> The nearest successful example (of collective denial) in the modern era is the 80 years of official denial by successive Turkish governments of the 1915-1917 genocide against the Armenians in which 1.5 million people lost their lives. This denial has been sustained by deliberate propaganda, lying, and cover-ups, forging documents, suppression of archives, and bribing scholars. Just as recent as 1974, secular and supposedly moderate Turkey invaded Cyprus, moved in Muslims, and ordered the Greeks to move out within 24 hours. Churches went up in flames or were converted into mosques.[10]

In Turkey today, Adolph Hitler's, *Mein Kampf* (My Struggle) is subsidized by the government and is one of the best selling books. Holocaust deniers and demonizers of the Jews are plentiful.

TURKEY'S TAKEOVER BY ISLAMISTS

In recent elections Recep Tayyip Erdogan became Prime minister and Abdulla Gul became President. These men represent the AKP Islamist party of Turkey. The outgoing President of Turkey had these words to say about the new administration:

> Turkey's political regime is under unprecedented threat—Political Islam is being imposed on Turkey as a model...A plot is being carried out, according to a well-defined timeline, against the Turkish Armed forces. Foreign forces—and domestic ones, to serve their own interests—are under the pretext of 'democracy,' trying to transform Turkey's secular republic and to create a model of a 'moderate Islamic republic' to serve as an example for Islamic countries

to follow. 'Moderate Islam' would mean that the state's social, economic, political, and legal system would reflect, to some extent, the laws of the religion. By this definition, the 'moderate Islam model' might represent 'progress' for the Islamic countries — but for Turkey, it means 'regression.' This model of 'fundamentalism' is one (that Turkey rejects).[11]

Erdogan expresses himself as being pro-democracy, pro-European, pro-American, pro-peace, and pro-global unity. However, he was caught saying, "Democracy is like a streetcar. You ride it until you arrive at your destination and then you get off."[12]

This leader of Turkey wrote this poem.

> The mosques are our barracks, (the) domes our helmets, the minarets our bayonets, (the) believers our soldiers. This holy army guards my religion. Almighty, our journey, our destiny, the end is martyrdom.[13]

Yet this man is a skillful politician, especially skilled in political manipulation. This fulfills another requirement for the leader of the Antichrist Kingdom.

John Hooper, a British journalist, wrote this concerning the implications of an Islamic Turkey: "The scope of conflict, were Turkey, like Iran, to 'go Islamic' would be immense." Commenting on this statement, Walid Shoebat made this statement:

> Nevertheless, if Turkey actually joins forces with Iran and several other Islamic countries, as the Bible says, then "immense" will not even begin to describe the devastating impact for Israel and the United States.[14]

TURKEY IN ISLAMIC PROPHECY

The first overthrow of Constantinople occurred in 1453 when the Muslims led by Mehmet II finally destroyed the Greco-Roman Empire. It does seem stranger than fiction but numerous Muslim traditions speak of a *second* conquering of Constantinople. This one is said to be by peaceful means just prior to the end of days. The Great War (Armageddon) as the Muslims call it will occur just after the peaceful conquest of Constantinople (Turkey). The tradition says:

> The flourishing state of Jerusalem will be when Yathrib (Medina) is in ruins, the ruined state of Yathrib will be when the Great War comes, and the outbreak of the Great War will be at the conquest of Constantinople when the Dajjal (Antichrist) comes forth. He (the prophet) struck his thigh or his shoulder with his hand and said: This is as true as you are here or as you are sitting.[15]

The conquest is, as we have seen, the take-over of Turkey by Islamists who hate Israel and the West.

The evidence for the fourth beast in Nebuchadnezzar's image being the Islamic Empire and the eighth and final kingdom being the revived Islamic Empire is now complete. In a few words, I want to try to sum up the premise that the Islamic Empire is the fourth beast and the revived Islamic Empire is the eighth kingdom.

First, the Roman Empire does not fulfill the requirements for several reasons:

- Rome never conquered the Babylonian and the Medo-Persian Empires.
- Rome's conquest does not agree with the nature of the fourth beast which "breaks in pieces and subdues all things." Rome was a builder; not a destroyer.

- The beast that comes out of the sea in Revelation 13:1, 2 was part leopard—Greece; part bear—Medo-Persia; and part lion—Babylonia. The Islamic Empire consists of all three. Rome does not.
- The eighth empire, the final empire "breaks in pieces and subdues all things." Rome (Europe) does not have the military to conquer the world. The European Union has outlawed capital punishment while the Antichrist's government beheads all the Jews and believers that refuse the mark of the beast. Demographics, a precise science, predicts the demise of Europe as we know it today.

Second, the Islamic Empire fits the bill, both scripturally and by current events unfolding before our eyes.

- The Islamic Empire that began with Mohammed and ended in the abolishing of the Ottoman Empire fits the description of breaking in pieces and subduing all things.
- The Islamic Empire conquered the Babylonian Empire, the Medo-Persian Empire, and the Greco-Roman Empire. Thus the beast of Revelation 13 was part leopard — Greece; part Bear — Medo-Persia; and part lion — Babylon is the Islamic Empire as it conquered all of these.
- Islam is gaining power every day. The West has turned its back on the Creator. God and especially Jesus Christ is an irritant to our society. The Great Apostasy is approaching and political correctness has a stranglehold on our media and government. Our President is a Muslim, and the FBI and the Homeland Security have been infiltrated with Islamist sympathizers.
- The caliphate movement is growing and Turkey will be the key player. The revived Islamic Empire will be the caliphate which will unite all Muslims for the final jihad that will lead to Armageddon.
- Mystery Babylon is Mecca and will be destroyed by the Muslim

Coalition. The Shi'as hate the Sunnis and resent Arab Imperialism. Before the battle of Armageddon, the Shiite coalition (Iran and Turkey) will undoubtedly nuke (atomic bomb) Mecca and Medina.

- According to Ezekiel 38, Joel 2, Micah 5, Zechariah 9, 12, and 14 and a host of other Scriptures, the Lord Jesus Christ will rescue Israel and with the raptured saints and the resurrected Tribulation saints will destroy the Muslim armies marching under the black flag army of the Mahdi.
- Any argument against the Mahdi being the Antichrist will not hold water. There is too much evidence both from Scripture and from the Muslim traditions.

I have studied these matters diligently, and I believe that what I have written in this book is true according to the Bible. Not only that, but the premises harmonize with the present situation and probable future events. In other words, the premises I have set forth pass both the correspondence test, i.e., true to the facts, and the coherence test, i.e., the premise is reasonable.

PART TWO

A BIBLICAL RESPONSE TO PROPHETIC TRUTH

Therefore, my beloved brethren, be ye steadfast, unmovable, always abounding in the work of the Lord, forasmuch as ye know that your labor is not in vain in the Lord.
1 Corinthians 15:58

CHAPTER FIFTEEN
A REALISTIC VIEW OF THE WORLD

Am I discouraged by learning the truth concerning the end times? Absolutely not! If our world were on an upward path, nations were at peace with one another, the world economy was booming, social problems were being eradicated, and millions were turning to Christ, etc., then our Bible would be unreliable. The Bible's prophecies coincide with what we observe on every hand. In Luke 18:8b, Jesus asks a rhetorical question implying a negative answer. *"Nevertheless when the Son of man cometh, shall he find faith on the earth?"* This indicates that "the faith," the body of Christian truth that we call the Christian faith, will be in short supply when our Lord returns.

Which churches are flourishing today? Even those churches that preach biblical truth, seek to stay unspotted from the world, and uphold old-fashioned Christian virtues are struggling to maintain the status quo. At the same time, those churches that have relaxed dress standards, relish contemporary Christian rock, and embrace the culture with social drinking, dancing and loose living cannot hold the crowds. Young people by the droves are leaving the church as soon as they are old enough to be on their own.

THE GREAT APOSTASY

The Bible plainly teaches that, in the last days, there will be a huge number of people who call themselves Christians turning away from the faith. Jesus speaks to this point in Matthew 24:10-

11, 24-25,
> *And then shall many be offended, and shall betray one another, and shall hate one another. And many false prophets shall rise, and shall deceive many. For there shall arise false Christs, and false prophets, and shall shew great signs and wonders; insomuch that, if it were possible, they shall deceive the very elect. Behold, I have told you before.*

More than likely, this prophecy relates to the Tribulation Period, and undoubtedly Islam is in the picture here. False prophets and deceivers will cause multitudes to turn from what might be called pseudo-Christianity" — Roman Catholic, Greek and Eastern Orthodox, and liberal Protestantism — to Islam. All true believers will have been raptured. When they see their Muslim neighbors worshipping the Beast, the Mahdi, they will cry out, *"Who is like the Beast? Who can make war against him?"* In other words, "If you can't beat them, join them."

What happens to those who refuse to join? Revelation 12:11 tells us: *"And they overcame him* (the Beast) *by the blood of the Lamb, and by the word of their testimony; and they loved not their lives unto the death."* Clearly, this is the proper context of this verse. Revelation 6:9 speaks of these overcomers. *"And when he had opened the fifth seal, I saw under the altar the souls of them that were slain for the word of God, and for the testimony which they held."* In Revelation 17:13, John has quite a bit to say about these martyrs who refused to apostatize.

> *And one of the elders answered, saying unto me, What are these which are arrayed in white robes? and whence came they? And I said unto him, Sir, thou knowest. And he said to me, These are they which came out of great tribulation, and have washed their robes, and made them white in the blood of the Lamb.*

2 Thessalonians 2:3 plainly predicts this move away from truth and virtue. *"Let no man deceive you by any means: for that day shall not come, except there come a **falling away** first, and that man of sin be revealed, the son of perdition."* In context, I believe the falling away mentioned in this verse occurs during the Tribulation Period, at the time when the "man of sin"—Antichrist—will be revealed.

CHURCH OF THE LAST DAYS DESCRIBED

1 Timothy 4:1 tells how the church will be seduced by the world and the culture toward the end of this age.

Now the Spirit speaketh expressly, that in the latter times some shall depart from the faith, giving heed to seducing spirits, and doctrines of devils; Speaking lies in hypocrisy; having their conscience seared with a hot iron.

2 Timothy 3:1-5 eloquently describes the breakdown of character and Christian values among professing Christians in the last days.

*This know also, that in the last days perilous times shall come. For men shall be lovers of their own selves, covetous, boasters, proud, blasphemers, disobedient to parents, unthankful, unholy, Without natural affection, trucebreakers, false accusers, incontinent, fierce, despisers of those that are good, Traitors, heady, highminded, lovers of pleasures more than lovers of God; Having **a form of godliness**, but denying the power thereof: from such turn away.*

STOCKHOLM SYNDROME

Joel Richardson in his book, *Islamic Antichrist*, writes about the "Stockholm Syndrome." Briefly, it is about the relationship between a captive and his captors. As a result of the captors showing mercy and not killing the captive, a feeling of gratitude and fear develops in the captive, and he becomes reluctant to display negative feelings toward the captors or terrorists. Eventually, the victim sees his captor as a "good guy," even a savior.[1]

This Stockholm Syndrome is at work in Israel. George E. Rubin writes in *Commentary Magazine*, May 2000, of what is happening to many in Israel.

> After fifty years of unending conflict, most Israeli Jews seem to have concluded that the burden of maintaining their nation is just too difficult to bear. The country's secular leftist elites — who control education, culture, the news media and the government — blame the Jews for the Arabs' desire to destroy Israel, and the majority seems to be afflicted with the Stockholm Syndrome. Though the victims of Arab hate, they identify with their oppressors.[2]

Islam is on the rise, and the countries of the West seem weak and unwilling even to admit that there is a clash of civilizations, and that jihad really exists. Our State Department, FBI, and Homeland Security are all being infiltrated by Islamophiles (those sympathetic to Islam). Political correctness demands that no criticism of Islam be tolerated. President Barack Obama said, "Let this point be very clear. We will not tolerate any negative stereotypes against Islam."[3] In the Muslim mind, anything Islam does is good and anything critical of Islam is bad.

As Islam gains power in non-Muslim lands, the Muslims will experience an emotional exhilaration. Contrariwise, non-Muslims will be gripped with fear as they witness Muslims increasing in numbers and influence. Most nominal Christians have little or no allegiance to Christ or to His church. Due to Muslim pressure, undoubtedly, many will turn to Islam.

PERSECUTION IS COMING

In John 15, Jesus tells us the world will hate His servants because it hated him. Jesus goes into a discourse on persecution and rejection and reminds us that the servant is not greater than his Lord. In John 16:1-3 our Lord looked down the corridors of time and saw what would happen to those that serve Him in the last days.

> *These things have I spoken unto you, that ye should not be offended. They shall put you out of the synagogues: yea, the time cometh, that whosoever **killeth you will think that he doeth God service**. And these things will they do unto you, because they have not known the father, nor me.*

In John 16:4 Jesus tells us why He is telling us these unpleasant things. "*But these things have I told you, that when the time shall come, ye may remember that I told you of them.*" We are not to be taken by surprise because Jesus told us before time what would happen.

MUSLIMS COMMANDED TO SLAY THE INFIDELS

Islam, with its jihad (holy war) — its policy of death to those who refuse to submit — seems to be in Jesus' mind. The Koran says in Surah 9:5,

> *So when the sacred months have passed away, then **slay the idolaters wherever you find them**, and take them captives and besiege them and lie in wait for them in every ambush,*

then if they repent and keep up prayer and pay the poor-rate, leave their way free to them; surely Allah is Forgiving, Merciful.

Ayatollah Ibrahim Amini justifies the slaughter of infidels in this way:

> This group (those who refuse to submit to Islam) will indisputably be opposed to justice and will never give up their stubborn antagonism against any power. Such people will do anything against the promised Mahdi to protect their vested interests. Moreover, they will do anything within their power to demoralize and combat those who support the Mahdi. To crush the negative influence of this group there is **no other solution except warfare and bloodshed.**[4]

PERSECUTION HAS BEEN THE NORM

According to Peter in his first epistle, Christians are called to suffer. 1 Peter 2:21 says, *"For even hereunto were ye called: because Christ also **suffered** for us, leaving us an **example**, that ye should follow his steps."* We seem to have difficulty comprehending the words of Jesus in the Sermon on the Mount as recorded in Matthew 5:10-12.

> *Blessed are they which are persecuted for righteousness' sake: for theirs is the kingdom of heaven. Blessed are ye, when men shall revile you, and persecute you, and shall say all manner of evil against you falsely, for my sake. Rejoice, and be exceeding glad: for great is your reward in heaven: for so persecuted they the prophets which were before you.*

If we glance back at history, we shall see that those who have stood for the Word of God have suffered. The early Christians were thrown to the lions in the Coliseum because their first loyalty was to Christ, not to Caesar. Thousands died during the Inquisition by the Roman Church for refusal to deny biblical doctrines. We are familiar with the Reformation martyrs in England who were burned at the stake for refusing to recant. Today, thousands daily risk imprisonment, torture and death for sharing their faith in Christ with others. These are the unsung heroes of which the world is not worthy. The liberal media has declared a blackout on persecution of Christians. To them it is not newsworthy! In 2009 in Nigeria hundreds of Christian homes were burned, churches torched, Christians killed and others forced to flee for their lives. Yet not one word of this grave injustice reached us through the major news media. In Islamic countries, Muslims kill Christians with impunity or no fear of consequences.

NO PERSECUTION, NO WITNESS

Persecution indicates spiritual life. Overt persecution is a sign of the failure of the persecutors. Failure to keep believers quiet leads to overt persecution – so overt persecution is an indication that believers have refused to be quiet. The lack of persecution results as believers keep their faith to themselves.

Nip Ripken in his article, "Recapturing the Role of Suffering," points out that suffering is an integral part of the normal Christian life. So when we hear of people being killed, imprisoned, abused for Christ what is our reaction to be? First, we should be thankful for these people of faith and courage who confidently witness for Christ knowing what awaits them. Instead of being sorry for them, we should praise God for them. Second, we should pray for them and for their loved ones to be strengthened as they suffer for Christ. Third, we should help them in practical ways, i.e., letters, visits and financial help.[5]

The number one cause of persecution is people giving their lives to Jesus and then witnessing to others of their new-found faith. If we pray for persecution to stop, if we pray that martyrs would only be a thing of the past, then we are praying for the effective work of God in hostile cultures to cease.

PERSECUTION AT MALUMGHAT HOSPITAL

Malumghat Hospital in southern Bangladesh became a target of Muslim persecution because a number of Muslims came to faith in Christ. A Muslim mob, led by their mullahs and imams, burned the homes of hospital employees and the Memorial Baptist Church. Fortunately, the Christians fled into the surrounding jungle and escaped. Five houses and the church were torched. Dr. John Sircar, president of the Bangladesh Theological Seminary and Bible College, made this comment: "They meant it for evil, but God meant it for good. The Christians rebuilt better, bigger houses and the new church was double the size of the old one. Do not feel sorry for us."

Here in America we do not yet face the loss of limb or life for sharing Christ with others. However, Christians who dare share their faith in the market place will endure suffering—not physical, but psychological and mental. Anyone who witnesses boldly for Christ will face pressure from unbelievers to desist. It could mean loss of job or rejection in other ways. The fear of embarrassment, rejection, loss of self-esteem is very real. In fact, it is so real it keeps the majority of Christians from actively sharing their faith.

PARADOX OF THE CROSS

I am afraid a "hothouse mentality" in our Christian walk and service has evolved. Personal peace (a life without crises) and personal prosperity (a life without want) dominate our prayers. Our emphasis has been upon ourselves: our salvation, our safety, our happiness. We have rejoiced in our sins being forgiven and the blessings of the riches in heavenly places with Christ, which is well and proper. Few, however, are willing to step out of their comfort zones to stand and witness for Christ.

Bob Sjogren in his article, "The Other Side of the Cross—Suffering and the Glory of God," speaks of two sides of the cross:

> One, as it relates to our sin; and second, as it relates to God's glory. Christ died for us that in turn we may live a life to the glory of God. Dying to sin, living for God, being an unashamed witness of His grace will certainly bring glory to God, but it will be accompanied by suffering.[5]

The world has never understood the cross and never will. 1 Corinthians 2:7-8 speaks of the mystery of the cross.

> *But we speak the **wisdom of God in a mystery**, even the hidden wisdom, which God ordained before the world unto our glory: Which none of the princes of this world knew: for had they known it, they **would not have crucified** the Lord of glory.*

Islam glories in conquest, besting their enemies, yes, and slaughtering them. The princes of this world (Rome and the Jewish High Priest) thought they were finished with this pestilent fellow, this rabble rouser called Jesus. After all, they killed him! But it was through suffering, the humiliation of the cross that God conquered His enemies and is glorified in all who are saved.

Without a doubt, hard times are coming for the people of God. Anyone telling you differently is a false prophet. My purpose in discussing the unpleasant subjects of suffering, defeat and death is not to scare or discourage God's people. This teaching is to prepare them for sure victory in what seems definite defeat.

Our Lord teaches this principle — victory in seeming defeat — so clearly in John 12:24-26.

> *Verily, verily, I say unto you, Except a corn of wheat fall into the ground and die, it abideth alone: but if it die, it bringeth forth much fruit. He that **loveth his life** shall lose it; and he that **hateth his life** in this world shall keep it unto life eternal. If any man serve me, let him follow me; and where I am, there shall also my servant be: if any man serve me, him will my Father honour.*

A corn of wheat (seed) that refuses to be buried and to die denies its purpose for existence. It abides alone and will finally perish. The seed that is buried and dies will find new life and fruitfulness. In God's program there is no success without suffering. Follow Christ wherever He leads and you will never be defeated.

CHAPTER SIXTEEN
WILL AMERICA BE ISLAMIZED?

Will America be Islamized? I mentioned in the Introduction that forty-nine years ago in Bangladesh, a Muslim cleric told me that one day Muslims would Islamize America. At that time, Islam was dormant; the thought of such a thing was ludicrous. Not so today. The fourth beast of Nebuchadnezzar's image of gold, described in Daniel 7:7 as *"dreadful and terrible, strong exceedingly with great iron teeth,"* the Islamic Empire, threatens our freedom and our way of life.

To understand the situation facing us, we need to consider some historical background concerning Islam. Mohammed was born in Saudi Arabia in 570 A.D. He and a few followers fled Mecca in 622 A.D. This flight was called the *hejira* or the "flight." The people of Medina welcomed Mohammed, accepting him as their religious, political and military leader.

Thus began the rise of the Islamic Empire. The fourth beast, the Islamic Empire, expired in 1924, slain by the Allied forces following World War I. This breakup resulted in the creation of Iraq, Jordan, Syria, Libya and other Middle Eastern countries.

BRIEF HISTORY OF THE CONFLICT

Struggle and strife define the relations between Christianity and Islam. The Caner brothers in their book, *Unveiling Islam,* point out seven momentous events in this struggle.

- Dome of the Rock Mosque erected in Jerusalem, 691 A.D.

- Great Mosque erected in Damascus, 715 A.D.
- Battle of Tours in France checks Islam's advance through Europe, 732 A.D.
- Crusades result in bitter relations between Islam and Christianity for future centuries, 1095-1291 A.D.
- Ottoman Turks capture Constantinople and the Byzantine Empire, 1453 A.D.
- Muslims driven out of Spain by Roman Catholics, 1492 A.D.
- Ottoman Empire joins forces with Kaiser Wilhelm of Germany, 1914-1918 A.D.[1]

RISE AND FALL OF ISLAM

Bernard Lewis, professor emeritus of Near Eastern Studies at Princeton University, sums up the attacks and counter-attacks, jihads and crusades, conquests and reconquests like this:

> For the first thousand years Islam was advancing and Christendom [was] in retreat and under threat. The new faith conquered the old Christian lands of the Levant (Middle East) and North Africa, and invaded Europe, ruling for a while in Sicily, Spain, Portugal and even parts of France. For the past three hundred years, since the failure of the second Turkish siege of Vienna, Austria, in 1683 and the rise of the European colonial empires in Asia and Africa, Islam has been on the defensive, and the Christian and post-Christian civilization of Europe and her daughters has brought the whole world, including, Islam, within its orbit.[2]

RESURGENCE OF ISLAM

Eleven years before the attack on the Twin Towers in New York City, Professor Lewis predicted in his article, "Roots of Islamic Rage," that trouble was on the horizon. According to his expectation, Muslims in great numbers have returned to their root proposition that the world lives in either the House of Islam or the House of Unbelief. From the Muslim standpoint, the greater part of the world is still outside Islam, and even inside the Islamic lands, according to views of Muslim radicals, the faith of Islam has been undermined and the law of Islam has been abrogated. The obligation of holy war begins at home and continues abroad, against the same infidel enemy.[3]

SAUDI INCURSION IN AMERICA

In the 1920s, with a growing concern about the depletion of domestic oil resources, Americans became junior partners of British, Dutch, and French oil companies. In 1933, Standard Oil of America signed an agreement with King Ibn Saud of Saudi Arabia. The American oil companies developed the Arabian and other Middle Eastern countries' oil fields, catapulting them into undreamed riches, power and influence. Shamefully, Franklin Delano Roosevelt gave this technology to the Arab countries with little or no return to the United States.[4] These Arab oil-producing nations now have the capability of blackmailing the industrial countries of the West. Only greed and love of money prevent them from cutting off our oil supply.

Now that the Islamic countries sit atop rich oil reserves, this economic power gives them once again the ability to renew their strategy of attacking unbelievers of any race, creed, color or background. This time it is not with frontal military assault, but with the force of terrorism seeking to break the will of the West to resist. Muslim terrorists learned that America under George W. Bush was not the "paper tiger" they imagined. The cold-hearted attacks on the World Trade Centers and the Pentagon united our country, resulting in an all-out war against terrorism. The fact that all 19 hijackers were from Saudi Arabia and surrounding Middle Eastern countries is significant.

HISTORY OF MODERN TERRORISM

Every movement has its foundation and guiding principles. The modern Islamic terrorist movement looks to Ibn Taymiyah, a powerful Sunni leader who was born in 1263. He set forth two principles that guide terrorists today.

- Muslims should resist, fight and overturn any Islamic government that does not govern the land according to the Islamic law only.
- Muslims should enforce jihad on anybody whose belief differs from Islam, especially Jews and Christians.[5]

WAHABBISM

Muhammad ibn Abd al-Wahab (1703-1792), using these principles, led the Wahabbi movement that resisted, fought and overturned the Turkish government. He established a new, 100 percent Islamic nation, which eventually became Saudi Arabia. Today the leadership of Saudi Arabia comprises many members of the original movement. Osama bin Laden is an example of that group[6]

MUSLIM BROTHERHOOD MOVEMENT

A spiritual leader, Sheikh Hassan al-Banna started the Muslim Brotherhood movement in Egypt. It was in protest of the secularization of Egypt, which followed the example of Turkey. The Muslim Brotherhood was very militant, aggressive, full of hatred toward their government and leadership. They used terrorist methods to shake up the country and pursue their agenda of bringing back the original glory of Islam. These terrorists focused their activities on assassination because they believed that killing was the only way to make Islamic nations resubmit to the Koran and the Islamic law.[7]

Sayyid Qutb, an Egyptian educatior and member of the Muslim Brotherhood, was born in 1906 and hanged by the Egyptian government in 1965. He has had a profound influence on Muslims worldwide through his book, *Signs along the Road.* Qutb is the philosopher and spiritual leader of today's terrorists. It is important for us to know his teachings. Here are a few of them:

- Americans excel in education, knowledge, technology, business, and civilization. However, the American values, ethics and beliefs are below the standard of a human being.
- There is no relation between the greatness of the culture and greatness of the people who create the culture. Americans have focused on materialism, but they don't have much to offer as to what makes humans great.
- Americans go to church on Sunday, Easter, Christmas and special religious occasions, yet they are so empty…no spiritual life.
- These heathen are not like the ones before Islam, but far worse. Today's heathen reverence and honor man-made constitutions, laws, principles, systems and humanistic methods. They disregard Allah's law and his constitution for life.
- We should immediately eliminate this pagan influence and the heathen pressure on our world. We must overturn this current society with its culture and leadership of infidels. Our first pri-

ority is to shake and change the foundations of heathens. We must destroy whatever conflicts with true Islam.[8]

AMERICA, BENEFICIAL BASE FOR TERRORISTS

Steve Emerson, investigative reporter, the author of *American Jihad: The Terrorists Among Us*, has been a champion for freedom as he documents and lists the cities and communities where these Islamists operate. Unbelievably, organizations such as Al-Queida, Hizballah, the Muslim Brotherhood, Algerian Armed Islamics, etc., have their offices in cities across our nation. Raleigh, North Carolina, is home to Islamic Jihad!

America has unwittingly provided these terrorist organizations with a safe haven where they can connect among themselves to further their nefarious purposes. Not only that, they have established non-profit religious, educational and charitable organizations which have raised millions of dollars to fund terrorism.[9]

Rachel Ehrenfeld in the *National Review*, November 1, 1993, exposed the Treasury Department's foolish and perhaps arrogant act of ignoring the law which required Treasury to designate assets held in the United States by terrorist countries and organizations. This is her report:

> Because Treasury has failed to implement the Grassley amendment, terrorists are able to raise funds and use them at will…The funds are usually smuggled out of the U.S., often in cash in large quantities, sometimes in gold. But not all the money collected in the U.S. ends up abroad. Some of it is used here to promote Muslim social services, build mosques, organize conferences, publish newsletters, and support terrorist activities. Allowing terrorist organizations and foundations to operate in the United States with impunity creates the obvious danger for US citizens.

Rewarding them with tax-exempt status adds insult to injury, forcing Americans to pay for their own endangerment through heavier tax burdens. No wonder, as Senator D'Amato commented in a recent interview, the 'terrorists are laughing at us.'[10]

AMERICA BIRTHS AL-QUEIDA AND THE TALIBAN

How can this be so? In 1986 William Casey, head of the Central Intelligence Agency (CIA), made the unwise decision to urge recruitment of radical Muslims from around the world to fight the Soviet Union in Afghanistan. Muslims from all over the world responded until they numbered over 100,000. They were given stinger missiles and military training. Along with that training, they were indoctrinated with the militant, orthodox Islamic doctrine known as Wahabbism.

They defeated Russia for sure. America soon lost interest in Afghanistan, but the *mujaheddin* Muslim fighters took over Afghanistan, and soon the Taliban were in control. Osama bin Laden, twenty-five years old, one of 51 children of a Yemeni businessman, represented Saudi Arabian interests in Afghanistan during the war. After the war, Osama organized Al-Queida (The Base) and turned Afghanistan into a training ground for Muslim terrorists. The rest is history.

AMERICA'S LAX SECURITY PROCEDURE

Bill Gertz, *Washington Times* investigative journalist, brings out shocking facts in his book, *Breakdown: How America's Intelligence Failure Led to September 11*. That the reader may be aware of our leaders' ineptness to protect us, I share the following:

- The CIA was not allowed to operate its intelligence gathering apparatus within the United States itself.
- Liberal Democrats in the Senate and the House set restrictions that inhibited the CIA and the FBI from being involved together in any intelligence gathering.
- The FBI was limited to crime-busting only. Spy-busting could not be on their agenda.
- The FBI and the CIA were politicized and promotions were not made based on operations experience.
- The FBI was barred from visiting websites of terrorist support organizations.
- FBI agents were forbidden to check websites of known terrorist organizations.
- The FBI was not allowed to attend any of the public meetings or conventions of these target groups.
- The FBI and the CIA were forbidden to cross over and share information with each other.[11]

What is behind this madness? Tony Blankley in his recent book, *The West's Last Chance*, asks such a question:

> Tolerance, the right to privacy, the right even to advocate sedition, and the right to equal protection under the law: The day is upon us when the West will have to decide which it values more: granting these rights and tolerance to those who wish to destroy us, or the survival of Western civilization. And this is another reason the West has been slow to react – because reacting violates its own values.[12]

Mr. Blankley offered more insight on what is going on in the security area. He made these remarkably salient observations in a recent column entitled "Governing Elites' Idiocy on Terrorism":

> ...There is a widening gap between public common sense

and governing class idiocy when it comes to spotting Islamist danger in our midst – and doing something about it.

...The slaughtered American troops at Ft. Hood are just among the early few in what will surely become whole legions of the dead victims of political correctness – if the public does not soon succeed at overruling the Western governing elite's unconscionable moral blindness to the malign danger in our midst.[13]

CHAPTER SEVENTEEN
WILL AMERICA BE ISLAMIZED? - CONTINUED

Something has gone terribly wrong. I read somewhere that a Muslim leader said, "Your freedoms will allow us to enslave you." What is wrong is that America is at war and does not know it. Jihad is working, and our leaders look the other way.

Daniel Pipes, expert on Islam and terrorism, reports that from 1979 until 2002, there were 55 Muslim terror attacks and 3,281 Americans killed in the United States.[1] In the report and investigation of the Fort Hood incident, Islam was mentioned only in a footnote! Political correctness will not permit publishing the blatant truth that Islam is behind the shootings, bombings and assassinations.

ISLAMISTS HAVE A PLAN TO DESTROY AMERICA

Muslims are not timid or secretive as to their intent to destroy us. One quote will suffice. I could give dozens. On February 3, 2005, Saudi cleric Musa al-Qarni during his weekly sermon said the following:

> The uproar and the chaos we see today in the human race – the killing, the acts of aggression, the rape, the robbery, and the disgrace of honor –what causes this is that the banners which are hoisted high are those of the Jews, the Christians, and other religions, and not the banner of "There is no god but Allah and Muhammad is Allah's Messenger"… First of all, we must realize that Allah obligated us to dis-

seminate this religion all over the globe...And Allah said, "Fight them until there is no more strife (resistance to Islam) and Allah's religion reigns supreme.[2]

Anis Shorrosh, Christian Arab from Jordan, won to Christ and discipled by Southern Baptist missionaries, has written a powerful book, *Islam Revealed – A Christian Arab's View of Islam.* In his Intelligence News Service G 2 Bulletin, he has listed 21 ways the Islamists will seek to capture America by 2020:

> 1. Agitate to create hate crime legislation so as to curb free speech in America when criticism is leveled at Islam.
> 2. Emphasize that Islam is the true religion for Afro-Americans, not Christianity.
> 3. Engage Americans in dialogue and discussions in schools and public forums, and insisting on the virtues of Islam and that "We worship the same God."
> 4. Nominate and support politicians sympathetic to Islam.
> 5. Buy controlling stock in newspapers, TV stations, radio stations, and motion picture corporations to influence media and popular culture.
> 6. Use oil as weapon, as 61% comes from the Middle East.
> 7. React violently when the Koran and Islam are criticized.
> 8. Encourage Muslims to aspire to positions of responsibility and power.
> 9. Accelerate Muslim growth in America by massive immigration and Muslim men marrying Christian women and having all the babies they can. 20,000 American women marry Muslims annually.
> 10. Develop an Islamic school system (Madrassas) to teach loyalty to the Koran and not the Constitution.
> 11. Give grants to American universities and colleges earmarked for Islamic studies and provide scholarships to bring Muslim students to America.

12. Teach that terrorists have hijacked Islam and Islam is really a peaceful, tolerant religion.
13. Portray Muslims in America as victims and immigrants from oppressed countries to create sympathy for them.
14. Manipulate the intelligence community with misinformation.
15. Threaten attacks that never happen.
16. Create riots in American prisons, insisting on shariah law instead of the American justice system, which is unfair.
17. Open scores of charities and use funds to support terrorists.
18. Insist freshmen on American campuses be taught a course on Islam by a Christian scholar sympathetic to Islam.
19. Coordinate Muslim efforts to propagate Islam with annual conventions and Internet connections.
20. Intimidate critics of Islam. Seek to eliminate them. Assassinate if necessary.
21. Applaud Muslims as hardworking, loyal Americans.[3]

This peaceful plan will not work because Americans value their freedoms and their faith too much to give in to shariah law. A current example: a Muslim professor at Vanderbilt University says homosexuals should be executed because that is shariah law and that is what he and all Muslims will follow. That went over like a turtle in a punchbowl! shariah law goes against everything our Constitution stands for.

OSAMA BIN LADEN'S SIX-POINT PLAN

Osama's plan does not take the peaceful route outlined above. Below is Osama's timetable to destroy America and the West:

- 2001: "The awakening" making Muslims worldwide aware that global jihad has begun.
- 2003-2006: "Opening the eyes" to make all Muslims aware of this global religious movement.
- 2007-2010: "Arising and standing up" to shake up secular Muslim governments, especially Pakistan and Saudi Arabia, and to undermine their stability.
- 2010-2013: Overthrow the secular Muslim governments, such as Egypt and Turkey, and replace them with Islamic republics.
- 2013-2016: Restore a united Islam caliphate that will be a world power.
- 2016-2020: Total war shall be declared between the Islamic caliphate and the rest of the nations of the world in the effort to impose Allah's law on the whole world. [4]

FIFTH COLUMN IN AMERICA

Emilio Mola Vidal, a Nationalist general during the Spanish Civil War (1936-39), originally coined the term "fifth column." As four of his army columns moved on Madrid, the general referred to his militant supporters within the capital as his "fifth column," intent on undermining the loyalist government from within.[5]

There is a "fifth column" in America, hating America, seeking to outlaw God, and aiding and abetting our sworn enemies, Islamic terrorists. They are the ACLU, the progressives, the socialists, the elite in our universities, the media, and the Democratic Party. Who but a "fifth columnist" would choose to prosecute evil-hearted terrorists in a civilian court instead of a military tribunal where they belong? Who but a "fifth columnist" would vote against the Patriot Act?

I would also suggest that there are quislings among us who would sell our heritage for a mess of pottage. The term, "quisling,"

– after Norwegian politician Vidkun Quisling, who assisted Nazi Germany to conquer his own country and ruled the collaborationist Norwegian government – is used to describe traitors and collaborators.[6] Leaders in our country are not fighting the enemies of our nation. But by political correctness, unjust judges, wrong interpretation of our laws, and other means, they are aiding and abetting those enemies. What these elite eggheads do not know is that if and when the Islamists win, their atheistic, liberal necks will be the first to feel the sword!

There is a definite loss of soul among these nihilists, humanists, atheists, secularists, multi-culturists and deniers of absolute truth. Jean Raspail, author of the *Camp of the Saints,* in his introduction speaks of this loss of soul:

> The West is empty, even if it has not become aware of it. An extraordinary inventive civilization, surely one capable of meeting the challenges of the third-millennium, the West has no soul left. At every level – it is always the soul that wins the decisive battles.[7] (Author's emphasis)

In such an atmosphere of unbelief, meaninglessness, immorality, and rebellion against God, Islam flourishes. Why? Because Islam has a **soul**, it has a **faith**, it has a **conviction**, it has a **will,** and it has a **claim**, i.e., "There is no god but Allah, and Muhammad is his Messenger." The Muslims believe it from the top of their heads to the tip of their toes.

WHAT CAN STOP ISLAM?

First, let me tell you what cannot stop Islam. 1) Bombs and bullets will not, because they love death just as much as we love life. 2) Democracy and diplomacy will not, because the rule of the people is as far from Islam as you can get. In Islam, government and religion are one and inseparable. 3) American dollars and rebuilding war-torn Muslim countries will not do it. They will give all credit to Allah and none to those that helped them.

Now let me tell you what can stop Islam. Churches – local churches with people filled with the Word of God and the Spirit of God, who love Jesus Christ more than they love their own lives – definitely can arrest Islam. Sad to say, the great majority of the Muslims in the world today have never met a Spirit-filled Christian.

Let me share a true story that fleshes out this truth. A Bangladeshi young man went to Kuwait to work in the oil fields so he could earn money and send it back to his family. While working in Kuwait, his foreman was an American Christian. This Christian man made such an impact on the young Muslim that when he returned to Bangladesh, he went to Malumghat Christian Hospital and met with a missionary. He announced that he wanted to become a Christian. When asked why he wanted to become a Christian, he answered, "I have seen one and I want to be like him."

Ah, my friend, the power of a Spirit-filled life! This Muslim man converted, was baptized, joined the church and became a full-time worker for the Lord. He did this at great risk of his life. His Muslim father was not at all happy with his son becoming a Christian, but confessed to him that he was a better man than his Muslim brothers.

Individually, or as one local church, our efforts may seem futile. Think with me for a minute of the remnant, i.e., all those who love Jesus sincerely, believe the Bible from cover to cover, and seek to obey the first two commandments of loving God and neighbors with all their hearts. You will find these people all over our country and all around the world. No one can know the power of the prayers of God's people as they repent of their sins and seek the God of heaven.

First, I would like to suggest what the remnant can do to retard Islam.

Pray. Down through history, prayer has moved the hand of

God time and time again. Without the storm that destroyed the Spanish Armada there very likely would have been no John Wesley, George Whitfield, or those Puritans that settled our shores. Pray for our national leaders – that they will understand the times, that they will have the courage to identify the enemy and the integrity to take appropriate action. Pray for our spiritual leaders – that they will cry to God for revival of God's people. Pray that the hearts of the fathers will be turned to their children and they will lead them in the right way. Please pray.

Evangelize. The Gospel is still the power of God unto salvation to all that will believe, Muslims included. Do not be a xenophobe (a fearer of foreigners), but reach out to them with friendship and follow on to give them the true Gospel.

Stand. When others want to compromise and take the easy way, stand for righteousness. Uphold biblical standards in our personal and church life. Never fear to own His Name.

Be involved. Stay active in your local church. Participate in local, state, and national government. For evil to win, all good men have to do is nothing.

WHAT CAN OUR GOVERNMENT DO TO STOP ISLAM

It does not take a Philadelphia lawyer to tell our government what they should do to protect us from those who would destroy our way of life and replace it with the ideas of a seventh century man claiming to be the last prophet of God. Let me give our government a few ideas that would make us all safer and help us to sleep better:

- Identify the enemy. Our enemy is not quiet or subversive. In speeches, pamphlets and books they reveal their intentions to destroy our country. All law enforcement people, FBI, CIA, Homeland Security and others, should arrest, prosecute, and

punish or deport all those who are found guilty of sedition and treason.
- Invade the mosques. Historically, in Islam the mosque is headquarters for jihad. Loyal Arabic speaking Americans should monitor what goes on. Muslims say one thing in English and something else in Arabic.
- Close down all terrorist headquarters and organizations and deport those who are disloyal to America and support jihad.
- Carefully monitor Islamic student groups on our college campuses.
- Close down terrorist training camps in our own country. There are over thirty in operation and nobody seems to care.
- Adopt a war-time mentality. Declare war on militant Islamists – those who are killing and attempting to blow up planeloads of innocent passengers are not criminals. They are terrorists. They are the enemy and should receive swift justice.
- Stop permitting Muslim schools to use textbooks filled with hate for Jews and Christians and contempt for our form of government.
- Confiscate the books and arrest those responsible. If foreigners, deport them.
- Profile when it will insure the good of our country and the safety of its citizens. No honest person minds being profiled. It is the guilty who scream.
- Stop immigration from Muslim countries. Why? Because Islam is not just a religion; it is a nationality. There is no separation of government and religion in Islam. If people are obligated to their religion and their religion does not fit our culture, then why let them come?
- Stop Muslim charities from funding those who are enemies of our state. Freeze their assets if found guilty.
- The prime purpose of government is to protect its citizens. Elect and support those who will protect us.

FINAL WORDS

There is so much more I could write about Islam and how it is affecting our country. Please do not think that I have animosity against any Muslim personally. I may not like what they say, what they write, or what they do. Yet I am commanded to love my enemies, which I seek to do.

Muslims are not our enemies. Islam, a devilish, clever religion, has captured the minds and hearts of over one billion people. Islam is the enemy. I can say that I honestly hate Islam, because as we have learned, it is antichrist from start to finish. Who could record the misery, the heartaches, the suffering this religion has inflicted on those not willing to yield?

In my ministry in Bangladesh, I had good relations with individual Muslims and Muslim families. They are human beings who love their children and have aspirations like us. So reach out to Muslims. Many of them are warm-hearted and are searching for truth, assurance and forgiveness. For the most part, one could say Muslims are good people trapped in a bad religion.

Around the world, thousands of Muslims are being saved. According to Walid Shoebat, many Muslims are turning to Christ:
In fact, the number of Muslims converting to Christianity is unprecedented. Many Christians who live in Muslim lands claim that what is taking place is nothing short of a Christian revival. Reports of high-level Imams converting to Christ are becoming commonplace. I believe with all my heart that the Middle East will see a genuine revival of Muslims coming to a biblical faith in Jesus.[8]

I have read of Iranian Christians bravely sharing their faith to the consternation of their persecutors. God is at work around the world, and in India, Africa and South America, multitudes are coming to Christ.

God's program is not set in stone. Prayer changes things. In the days of Sodom, God promised Abraham if ten righteous people could be found, He would spare that wicked city (Genesis 18:32).

Then in Exodus, when God was determined to destroy Israel and make a new nation of Moses, the intercession of Moses stayed God's hand. Can we forget Jonah and Nineveh? Jonah's message was "forty days and Nineveh will be destroyed." At the preaching of that unwilling prophet, the city repented and was spared. The fact that the situation is grim should spur us to pray to God for a great deliverance.

In the Introduction I mentioned that God called me to preach the Gospel 59 years ago. As a result of hearing Biblical teaching on sin and salvation, I repented of my sins and received Jesus Christ as my personal Savior and Lord. I experienced a dramatic change. I was born again and began a new life of fellowship with God. Sinful habits dropped off as dead leaves fall off a tree. A hunger for God and His Word filled my life. God and His Word have been my satisfying portion these 59 years.

What power changed a sinful, lustful, pleasure-seeking, purposeless young man into a preacher of the Gospel? Let me briefly share the Gospel with those who have read this book.

- The God of creation is the God of salvation.
- God made all things good. *"And God saw every thing that he had made, and, behold, it was very good"* (Genesis 1:31).
- Man (Adam and Eve) rebelled against God. *"Wherefore, as by one man sin entered into the world, and death by sin; and so death passed upon all men, for that all have sinned"* (Romans 5:12).
- God's holiness demands death for sin. *"The wages of sin is death"* (Romans 6:23)
- Christ died for our sins. *"For Christ also hath once suffered for sins, the just for the unjust, that he might bring us to God"* (1 Peter 3:18).
- Confess and believe. *"That if thou shalt confess with thy mouth the Lord Jesus, and shalt believe in thine heart that God hath raised him from the dead, thou shalt be saved"* (Romans 10:9).
- Receive Christ as your Savior and Lord. *"But as many as received*

him, to them gave he power to become the sons of God, even to them that believe on his name" (John 1:12).

Whoever you are, whatever you may have done or said, Jesus Christ invites you to come to Him. *"Come unto me, all ye that labour and are heavy laden, and I will give you rest. Take my yoke upon you, and learn of me; for I am meek and lowly in heart: and ye shall find rest unto your souls. For my yoke is easy, and my burden is light"* (Matthew 11:28-30).

Trust Him, and you can say with the Psalmist, *"Give us help from trouble: for vain is the help of man. Through God we shall do valiantly: for he it is that shall tread down our enemies"* (Psalm 108:12-13).

THE END

END NOTES

CHAPTER 1

1. *Islam and Christianity*: A Muslim and a Christian in Dialogue, pp. 30-31.
2. en.wikipedia.org/wiki/hadith

CHAPTER 2

1. http://wikipedia.org/Mahdi/history
2. Islamicweb.com/history/mahdi.htm
3. http://wikipedia.org/Mahdi/history
4. en.wikepedia.org/wiki/Mahdi#Muslim_beliefs_common_to_both_Sunnis_and_Shias
5. http.//en.wikipedia.org.wiki,Muhammad al-Mahdi
6. Ibid.
7. inshad.org/Islam/Prophecy/Madhi.htm
8. ibid.
9. ibid
10. ibid
11. Richardson, Joel, *The Islamic Antichrist, The Shocking Truth about the Real Nature of the Beast*, WND Books, Los Angeles, CA, 2009, p.28.
12. ibid. p. 29.
13. Mishkaat, p. 471.
14. Albidaayah, vol,6 p. 184.
15. Tirmidhi as quoted in Zubair, Signs of Qiyamah, p. 42.
16. Izzat and Arif, *Al Mahdi and the End of Time*, p. 40.
17. Sahih Muslim Book 041, Number 6985.

18. Sahih Hakim Mustadrak, related by Abu Sa'id al-Khudri, 4:557 and 558 as quoted in Kabbani.
19. Al-Tabarani, related by Abu Huraya, as quoted in Izzat and Arif, *Al Mahdi and the End of Time,* p. 9.
20. Izzat and Arif, p. 40.
21. ibid.
22. Richardson, pp. 31, 32.

CHAPTER 3

1. en wikipedia.org/wiki/antichrist

CHAPTER 4

1. Walid Shoebat, *God's War on Terror – Islam, Prophecy and the Bible,* Top executive Media, 2008, p. 60.
2. Ibn Khaldun, *The Muqaddimah*, translated by Franz Rosenthal (New York Pantheon Books Inc.) Vol. 1:473.
3. Shoebat, p. 65.
4. Ahmad ibn Naqib al Misri, *The Reliance of the Traveller*, translated by Nun Ha Mim Keller (Amana Publications, 1997) section 18.2, page 745.
5. Madiwatch.org
6. Sahih Hakim Mustadrak, 4:557,558.
7. Richardson, p. 29
8. Islam 101, *Religion of Peace*, Robert Spencer, Washington, DC, Regency Publishing , inc. p. 165.
9. Armstrong, Karen, *Islam, a Short History,* Random House, New York, 2002, p.16.
10. U.S. Department of state report on *Human Rights Practices in Saudi Arabia.*
11. Shoebat, p. 91.

CHAPTER 5

1. Md. Ibn 'Izzat and Md. 'Arif, *Al-Mahdi and the End Times*, p. 44.
2. Ibid., p. 40.
3. Ibid.
4. *Sahih Muslim Book* 041, Number 6985.
5. Shoebat, p. 92.
6. Sperry, Paul, U.S – *Saudi Oil Imports Fund American Mosques*, Worldnet Daily, April 22, 2002, p. 2.
7. Shoebat, p. 97.
8. http://iisca.org/knowledge/jihad_for_allah.htm
9. Ibn Khaldun, *The Muqqaddimah*, trans. By Franz Rosenthal (New York: Pantheon Books Inc., 1958) Vol. 1473.
10. www/http:/en.wiki.org/First Crusade
11. Fruchtenbaum, "*Nationality,*" pp. 17,18. From article by Thomas Ice, *The Ethnicity of the Antichrist,* May 8th 2007, Prophetic News.

CHAPTER 6

1. Narrared Abu Bin Malik, *Hadith Sahih Bukhari,* vol.1 #387.
2. Tabarani, as related by Hadrat Abu Umamah, as quoted by Zubair Ali, p. 43 and Abduallah, p. 55.
3. Joel Richardson, *The Islamic Antichrist, The Shocking Truth about the Real Nature of the Beast,* WND Books, Los Angeles, CA, 2009, p.28
4. Michelle Malkin, blog.
5. http://www.omudan.org/hudna, htm
6. Jihad in Islam by Sayyeed Abdul a la Maududi Islamic Publication (Pvt) Ltd. p..8.
7. Shoebat, p. 138
8. Tafsir Ibn Kathir; Al-Baqarah
9. World Magazine, November 21, 2009, p. 52

10. wikipedia.org/wiki/guillotine
11. en,wikipedia.org/wiki/Nick_Berg
12. en,Wikipedia.org/wiki/Daniel_Pearl
13. www.meforum.org/713/beheading in the name of Islam.
14. Ibid.
15. Ibid.

CHAPTER 7

1. Albert Speer, (1905-1981), Nazi Germany's Minister for Armaments 1942-1945).
2. Ibid.
3. Ibid.
4. Marvin Olsaky, World Magazine, October 23, 2004, p. 52.
5. *The Waffen SS* by George Steinll, 1966, p. 52.
6. Sahih Muslin Book 041, Number 6985.
7. Muhammad Ali Ibn Zubair, *The Signs Qiyama*, translated by M. Azal Hoosein Elias.
8. http:///members.cox.net/arshad/qiyama.html.
9. Muhammad ibn Izzat and Muhammad 'Arif, p. 40.
10. Saudis put bodies of beheaded Sri Lankans on display. Ethan McNern, Scotsman.com February 21, 2007.
11. Shayk Muhammad Hisham Kabbani, *The Approach of Armageddon? An Islamic Perspective*, (Canada, Supreme Muslim Council of America, 2003, p. 223.
12. Excerpts from a sermon by Palestinian Authority Imam Sheikh Ibrahim Mahdi at the Sheikh Ijlin Mosque in Gaza City broadcast live on April 12, 2002.

CHAPTER 8

1. Richardson, p. 58, 59.
2. Kabbani, p. 238.
3. Richardson, p. 69.
4. Keen, Charles, Editor, *Unpublished Word,* Fall, 2009, p. 17.

CHAPTER 9

1. http:/en,wikipedia.org.wiki/Dajjal#Islam27/description.
2. http:/en,wikipedia.org/wiki.Dajal.
3. http://wikipedia.inter-islam.org/faith/Dajjal.htm
4. Ibn Maja, Kitab al-Fitan 44084, quoted in Kabbani, *The Approach of Armageddon?* p. 231.
5. www.inter-islam.org/faith/Dajjal.htm
6. Shafi and Usmani, *Signs of the Qiyamma and the Arrival of the Maseeh,* p. 60.
7. Kabbani, *Approach of Armageddon,* p. 237.
8. Sunan Abu Dawood, Book 37, number 4310, narrated by Abu Hurayrah.

CHAPTER 10

1. Living an Apologetic Life, Just thinking, Zacharias, Ravi. Fall 2003, p. 3.
2. Islamic Antichrist, Richardson, pp. 82,83.
3. Ibid., p. 88.89.
4. Why I Left Jihad, Shoebat, www. Shoebat.com; Islam and the Final Beast, http://www.answering-islam.org/Walid/gog.htm
5. *Complete Commentary on the Whole Bible,* Henry, Matthew
6. *God's Prophetic Blueprint,* Shelton, Bob Jones Press, Greenville, pp. 55,56.
7. Shoebat, p. 257.
8. Ibid., 272

CHAPTER 11

1. *The Beast and the End Times Events,* Zomaya, Solomon p. 25.
2. En.wikipedia.org/wiki/Ottoman_Empire.
3. Shoebat, p. 312.
4. Justin' *History of the World* as cited in Trogus Pompeius, in Justin, Cornelius Nepos and Eutropios. John Selby Watson,tr. (London: George Bell and Sons, 1876) pp. 272   -283.
5. Shoebat. pp.. 31
6. *Daniel, a New Translation with Commentary Anthologized from Talmudic, Mishradic, and Rabbinic Sources,* Mesora Publication (Brooklyn, NY, 1969), p. 104.
7. Wesley, John, *The Doctrine of Original Sin Works,* 1841.
8. Anderson, Sir Robert, *The Coming Prince, The Ten Kingdoms,* pp. 273,276.
9. Edwards, Jonathan, *The Fall of Antichrist,* Part VII, New York Publishers, 1829, p. 395.
10. Ibid., p. 399.
11. Shoebat. p. 331.
12. Sheen, Archbishop J. Fulton, 1952 in the Mindzenty Report and reprinted in 2001 by the Cardinal Mindzenty Foundation.
13. Steyn, Mark, America Alone, pp. xv,xvi
14. http://www.brusselsjournal.com/node/1609.

CHAPTER 12

1. www.gotquestions.org/day-of-the-Lord.html.
2. Rodison, Maxine, *Muhammad,* Pantheon Books, New York, 1971, p.213 and Warraq, Ibn, *Why I Am Not a Muslim,* Promotheus

Books, Amherst, NJ, 1995, p.96.
3. Shoebat, p. 188.
4. Ibid., 204.
5. Balfour Declaration of 1917,Wikipedia the free encyclopedia.

CHAPTER 13

1. Solomon, p. 48.
2. Lewis, Bernard, *The Arabs in History*, p. 15 B.L., London, 1947.
3. Shoebat p. 396.
4. Paul Sperry, *U.S. Saudi Oil Imports Fund American Mosques*, Worldnetdaily, April 22, 2002, p.2.
5. Shoebat. p. 407.
6. Yawm Al-Ghadah, Safar Alhwaly
7. Narrated Mu'adh ibn Jabal: Translation of Sunan Abu -Dawud, *Battles (*Kitab Al-Malahim), Book 37, Number 4281.
8. Trivocic, Serge, *The Sword of the Prophet—Islam History, Theology, and Impact on the World,* Regina Orthodox Press, Boston, MA, s00s, p. 246.
9. Shoebat. p. 410.

CHAPTER 14

1. En.wikipedia,org/wiki/Kaliph
2. Shoebat, p. 450.
3. Jihadwatch.org April 16, 2006.
4. Gabriel, Mark, *Islam and Terrorism –What the Koran really teaches about Christianity, violence, and the goals of Islamic jihad,* Charisma House, Lake Mary, FL., 2001, p. 72.
5. Shoebat, p. 430.
6. *Global Politician Turkey as Mediator and Peackeeper during Middle East Conflict: Analyzing Events of summer 2006,* Professor Ruben

Safrastyan, Ph.D, 6/13/2007.
7. World Magazine, "Switching Sides," November 2009, p. 52.
8. Ibid.
9. Dale Foster, *Business and Economic Development in Turkey*, July 15, 2007.
10. Stanly Cohen, Professor of Criminology, Hebrew University, *Law and Social Inquiry*, vol. 20, no. 1, winter, 1995, pp. 7 and 50.
11. The Middle East Media Research Institute Blog, *Turkish President Strongly Warns: Turkish Republic in Danger from Within*. Htt://www.thememriblog.org/blog_personal/en/1214.htm
12. http://www.groundreport.com/articles.php?id=2834027.
13. Ibid.
14. Shoebat. p. 442.
15. Sunan of Abu-Dawood Book 37: Number 4281 Narrated by Mu'ah ibn Jabal.

CHAPTER 15

1. Richardson, Joel, p. 167.
2. Rubin, George E., Commentary Magazine, *Letters*, May, 2000.
3. http://www.youtube.com.watch-popup
4. Amini, Al-Imam Al Mahdi, *The Just Leader of Humanity*.
5. Ripken, Nik, *Recapturing the Role of Suffering*, Mission Frontiers, January-February, 2010, p. 7.
6. Sjogren, Bob, *The Other side of the Cross*, Mission Frontiers, January-February, 2010, p. 7.

CHAPTER 16

1. Caner, Ergin and Emir, *Unveiling Islam – An Insider's Look at Muslim Life and Beliefs*, Kregel Publications, Grand Rapids, MI, 2002, p. 72.

2. Lewis, Bernard, *The Roots of Islamic Rage,* Atlantic Monthly, September, 1990, pp. 47-60.
3. Caner, p. 67.
4. Ramatai, Yohanan, *The Islamic Danger to Western Civilization,* Special Publication of the Jerusalem Institute for Western Defense, 2002, p. 4, 5.
5. Gabriel, Mark, p. 111.
6. Ibid., p. 112.
7. Ibid., pp. 113, 114.
8. Ibid., pp. 115 – 119.
9. Emerson, Steve, *American Jihad: The Terrorists Among Us* (New York: The Free Press, 2002).
10. Ehrenfeld, Rachel in the National Review, November 1, 1993.
11. Gertz, Bill, *Breakdown: How America's Intelligence Failure Led to September 11.*
12. Blankley, Tony, *The West's Last Chance.*
13. Blankley, Tony, *Governing Elites' Idiocy on Terrorism,* e-mail from ACT FOR AMERICA, February 2, 2010.

CHAPTER 17

1. Pipes, Daniel, *New York Times,* 2002.
2. Sermon by Musa al-Qarni in Saudi Arabia, February 3, 2005.
3. Shorosh, Anis, Intelligence News Service G 2 Bulletin.
4. Murk, Jim, *Islam Rising – The Never Ending Jihad Against America and the West,* 21st Century Press, Springfield, MO, 2009, p. 195.
5. en.wikipedia.org/fifthcolunmns,wiki.com
6. en.wikipedia.org/quisling.wiki.com
7. Raspail, Jean, *Camp of the Saints,* The Social Contract Press, Petoskey, MI, 1973, p. xv.
8. Shoebat, p. 467.

GLOSSARY

Abu Bakr — First Caliph (Muslim Ruler) in Mecca
Ali — Son-in-law of the Prophet Mohammed; married the Prophet's daughter, Fatima; first Imam (leader) of the Shi'ite sect.
Allah — Arabic name for God
Allahu Akbar — "God is great"
Armageddon — The last great battle
Ayatollah — Head religious leader of the Shi'ites
Caliph — Leader of the Muslim Coalition
Caliphate — Coalition of Muslim nations ruled by a Caliph
Dajjal — The Christian Messiah who will oppose the Mahdi
Dar-al-Harb — "House of War"; areas of world unconquered by Islam
Dar-al-Islam — "House of Islam"; territory under Muslim control
Gabriel — Angel that communicated the Koran to Mohammed
Hadith — Traditions; the recorded words, actions, and attitudes of the Prophet Mohammed.
Hajj — Pilgrimage to Mecca
Hajji — One who has made pilgrimage to Mecca
Hegira — The flight of Mohammed and his followers to Medina. Beginning of Muslim calendar –A.D September 20, 622
Hudna — A peace treaty for the purpose of gaining advantage in a future conflict
Imam — Leader of the Mosque
Iman — Faith, belief and doctrines of a religion
Jihad — Efforts to extend or defend the faith of Islam
Kabah — "Cube"; holy building in Mecca
Kafir — Infidel, non-believer
Khadijah — First wife of Mohammed
Khalifa — Caliph, successor of Mohammed

Khalifat — Caliphate
Koran — "Recitations" Mohammed received from angel Gabriel
Madrasa — Islamic religious school
Masjid — Mosque; where Muslims congregate to pray
Mecca — Birthplace of Mohammed; site of Kabah, destination of pilgrimage
Medina — Arabian city that welcomed Mohammed; location of his tomb
Muslim — One who submits to Allah and confesses Mohammed to be his prophet
Mullah — Leader of the mosque
Nasek — Later portion of the Koran abrogating an earlier portion
PBUH — Peace be upon him, always mentioned after the name of Mohammed and other prophets
Qur'an — Variant spelling of Koran
Ramadan — Ninth month of Muslim year; the month of the fast
Rasul — Messenger or apostle; title of Mohammed
Shahada — Confession; :There is no god but Allah, and Mohammed is his Messenger.
Shahid — Martyr
Shari'a — Muslim rule or law
Shi'ite — Minority Muslim community that accepted Ali as the successor of Mohammed
Sheik — A religious leader; title of respect
Shirk — Unpardonable sin of associating anything or any person with Allah
Sunnah — Orthodoxy; the true path of Islam
Sunni — Major Muslim community; claim to be orthodox
Twelver Shi'as — Believe the 12th Imam is the Mahdi
Ummah — The world-wide Muslim community
Wahabi — Militant sect of Islam; founded by al Wahab in Arabia in A.D. 1703-92
Zakat — Almsgiving; 1/40 of income

BIBLIOGRAPHY

A Cup of Trembling — Jerusalem and Bible Prophecy, David Hunt, Harvest House Publishers, Eugene Or. 1995.

American Jihad – The Terrorists Living Among Us, Steven Emerson, The Free Press, New York, 2002.

Answering Islam, The Crescent in Light of the Cross, Norman Geisler and Abdul Saleeh, Baker Books, Grand Rapids, MI, 2002.

Behind the Veil — Unmasking Islam, Abd el Schafi, Pioneer Book Company, Caney, KS, 2001.

Fast Facts on the Middle East Conflict, Randall Price, Harvest House Publishers, Eugene, OR. 2003.

God's War on Terror — Islam, Prophecy and the Bible, Walid Shoebat,
Top Executive Media, 2008.

Hamas VS. Fatah – The Struggle for Palestine, Johathan Schanzer, Palgrave Macmillan, New York, 2008.

Inside Islam, Exposing and Reaching the World of Islam, Reza Safa, Charisma House, Lake Mary, FL. 1996.

Islamic Antichrist — The Shocking Truth about the Real Nature of the

Beast, Joel Richardson, WND Books, Los Angeles, CA, 2009.

Islam — a Short History, Karen Armstrong, the Modern Library, New York, 2000.

Islam, a User Friendly Guide, Bruce Bickel and Stan Jantz, Harvest House Publishers, Eugene, OR, 2002.

Islam and Christianity, Donald Tingle, Inter-Varsity Press, Madison, WI. 1985.

Islam and the Jews —t he Unfinished Battle, Mark Gabriel, Charisma
House, Lake Mary, FL. 2003.

Islam and Terrorism — What the Quran Really Teaches About Christianity, Violence and the Goals of the Islamic Jihad, Mark Gabriel, Charisma House, Lake Mary, FL. 2002.

Islam in History — Ideas, People, and Events in the Middle East, Bernard Lewis, Open Court, Chicago and La Salle, IL, 1993.

Islam: Its Prophet, Peoples, Politics and Power, George Braswell, Jr., Broadman and Holman Publishers, Nashville, TN. 1988.

Islam Revealed — A Christian Arab's View of Islam, Anis Shorrosh, Thomas Nelson Publishers, Nashville, TN. 1988.

Islam Rising —The Never Ending Jihad Against Christianity, Book One, *Islam Rising — The Never Ending Jihad Against the Jews and Israel,* Book Two, *Islam Rising — The Never Ending Jihad Against America and the West,* Book Three, Jim Murk, 21st Century Press, Springfield MO, 2006, 2007, 2009.

Islam Unveiled — Disturbing Questions About the World's Fastest Growing Faith, Robert Spencer, Encounter Books, Sans Francisco, CA, 2002.

Islamic Invasion — Confronting the World's Fastest Growing Religion,
Robert Morey, Christian Scholars Press, Las Vegas, NV. 1992.

Jesus, Prophecy and Middle East, Anis Shorrosh, Acclaimed Books, Dallas, TX. 1979.

Jesus Vs. Jihad, Exposing the Conflict Between Christ and Islam, Marvin Yakos, Charisma House, Lake Mary, FL. 2001.

Leaving Islam — Apostates Speak Out, Ibn Warraq, Prometheus Books, Amherst, NY. 2003.

Light and Shadow of Jihad — the Struggle for Truth, Ravi Zacharias, Multnomah Publishers, Sisters, OR. 2002.

Milestones, Sayyid Qutub, Mother Mosque Foundation, Cedar Rapids, IA.

Militant Islam Reaches America, Daniel Pipes, W.W. Norton and Company, New York, 2002.

Muslim Mafia — Inside the Secret Underworld that's Conspiring to Islamize America, David Gaubatz, WND Books, Los Angeles, CA, 2009.

Now They Call Me Infidel — Why I Renounced Jihad for America, Israel, and the War on Terror, Nonie Darwish, Penguin Books, New York, 2006.

One God One Message, Discover the Mystery, Take the Journey,

P.D. Bramsen, Rock international, Greenville, SC, 2007.

Reaching Muslims for Christ, William Saal, Moody Press, Chicago, IL, 1991.

Secrets of the Koran, Don Richarson, Regal Books, Ventura, CA, 2003.

Share Your Faith With A Muslim, C. R. Marsh, Moody Press, Chicago, IL, 1991.

The Bible and Islam, Bassam Madany, Back to God House, Palos Heights, IL. 1992.

The Complete Idiot's Guide to Understanding Islam, Yahiya Emerick, Alpha Books, Indianapolis, IN, 2002.

The Complete Infidel's Guide to the Koran, Robert Spencer, Regnery Publishing, Washington, D.C., 2009.

The Crisis of Islam — Holy War and Unholy Terror, Bernard Lewis, The Modern Library, New York, 2003.

The Crucifixion of Christ: A Fact or Fiction — A Reply to Crucifixion or Crucifiction, John Gilchrist, Muslim Friendship Ministries, Ontario, Canada, 1994.

The Decline and Fall of the Roman Empire, Edward Gibbon, Harcourt, Brace and Company, A One Volume Abridgment by D.M. Low, New York, 1960.

The Holy Injil — First Book of Matthew, IBS Publishing, Colorado Springs, CO, 2001.

The Liberated Palestinian — The Anis Shorrosh Story, James and Marti Hefley, Victor Books, Wheaton, IL, 1975.

The Life of Muhammed, Md. Husayn Haykal, New Crescent Publishing Company, Delhi, India, 1976.

The Muslims of America, Edited by Yvonne Yazbeck Haddad, Oxford University Press, New York, 1991.

The Oxford History of Islam, John Exposito, Oxford University Press, New York, 1999.

The Peril of Islam — Telling the Truth, Gene Gurganus, Truth Publishers, Greenville, SC, 2004.

The Qu'ran, Translated by Richard Bell, T & T Clark, Edinburg, 1937.

The Sword of the Prophet — Islam History, Theology, Impact on the World, Serge Trifkovic, Regina Orthodox Press, Boston, Ma, 2002.

Understanding Some Muslim Misunderstandings, Ernest Hahn, Fellowship of Faith for the Muslims, Toronto, Canada, 2001.

The Way of Righteousness — Good New for Muslims, Paul Bramsen, CMML, Spring Lakes, NJ, 1998.

Unveiling Islam — An Insider's Look at Muslim Life and Beliefs, Ergun and Emir Caner, Kregel Publications, Grand Rapids, MI, 2002.

What Is the Religion of Islam? Henry Pike, Silent Word Ministries,

Trenton, GA, 2001.

What You Need to Know About Islam and Muslims, George W. Brawell, Jr., Broadman and Holman Publishers, Nashville, TN, 2000.

Who Is This Allah? G.J.O. Moshay, Dorchester House Publications, Gerrard Cross, United Kingdom, 1985.

Why I Left Islam, Ibn Warraq, Prometheus Books, Amherst, NY, 1985.

Women in Islam, P. Newton and M. Rafiqui Haqq, The Berean Call, Bend, OR, 1995.

PERSONAL INDEX

Elizabeth Jeannette English Gurganus iii
Clayton Shumpert .... vii,x
Walid Shoebat vi,viii,0,41,58,77,84,110,111,114,118, 120,134,140,145,155,158,163,195
Joel Richardson vi,viii,20,23,50,64,73,84,90,93, 109,115,118,170
Mark Gabriel viii,156,173,198
Jim Murk viii,213
Martha Knox viii
Jerry Gass viii
Bob Nestor viii
Lydia Gurganus Greene viii
Jay Walsh viii
Jim Bailey viii
Clayton Shumpert viii
Bill Kinkade viii
Dick Knox viii
Jess Easton viii
Jim Starr viii
Nonie Darwish viii
David Horowitz viii
Anish Shorrosh viii,188
Steve Emerson viii,183
Danie Pipes viii,187
Aaron Greene v
Caleb Greene v
Zach Fransen v
Gene Gurganus v

PERSONAL INDEX **215**

Kaddafi	xii
B.D. Kateregga	3
Abu Bakr	13
Ali, Son in law of Mohammed	13
Moojan Momen	15,16
Hasan al-Askari	17
Hujjat ibn al-Hasan	17
Hadrat Abdullah bin Mas'ood	18
Hadrat Abu Umamah	20, 64,73
Ka'b –Ahbar	20,23, 47
Ad-Dani	23
Hitler	26, 33, 76, 77
Mussolini	26
Stalin	26
Gorachev	26
John Fitzgerald Kennedy	26
Barack Husain Obama	26, 104
Abdullah Al-Ghazali	45
Karen Armstrong	49
Abu Qanit al-Sharif al Hasani	50
Ibn Khaldun	60
Ahmad ibn Naqi al Misri	50
Franklin Delano Roosevelt	53, 180
Pope Urban II	59
Md. Ibn Izzat	60,80
Md. Arif	60,80
Fruchtenbaum	61
Ayatollah Khomeini	64,149
Pat Roberson	65
Bill O'Reilly	65
Michelle Malkin	65,73
Shira A. Drissman	66
Malawna Sayid Abul Ala Mawdudi	67
Abdul Rahman al Wahabi	68

Caroline Glick	68
Nicholas Evan Berg	70
Daniel Pearl	70
Imam Muhammad Adam al Sheik	71
Sam Hamod	71
Albert Speer	77
Adolph Hitler	26,77,162
Heinrich Himmler	78
Sheik Kabbani	83,92,96,102
Charles Keen	93, 96
Osama Abdallah	100
Ravi Zacharias	107
Matthew Henry	110,118
C. I. Scofield	110
Zomoya Solomon	14,116,130,139
Mehmet II	117,125,161
Osman I	117
Justin	118,130
Ibn Ezra	120
John Wesley	120
Sir Robert Anderson	121
Jonathan Edwards	121
Bishop Fulton Sheen	122
Mark Steyn	123
Henryk M. Broder	124
Harry Truman	138
Bernard Lewis	8, 141,179,180
Saddam Hossain	149
Yusuf al-Qaradawi	152
Osama bin Laden	152,181, 184,189
Sheik Ismail Nawahda	155
Sheik Raed Salah	155
Alexander the Great	158

Antiochus IV Epiphanes 158
Mustafa Kemal Ataturk 159
Ruben Safrastyan 159
Recep Tayyip Ergodan 160, 161, 163
President Ahmadinejad 160
Stanley Cohen 162
Abdulla Gul 162
John Hooper 163
George E. Rubin 171
John Sircar 175
Ayatola Ibrahim Amini 173
Nik Ripken 174
Bob Sjogren 176
Ergin and Emir Caner 178
Kaiser Wilhelm 179
King Ibn Saud 180
George W. Bush 190
Ibn Taymiyah 181
Abd-al-Wahab 181
Sheik Hassan al-Banna 182
Sayyid Qutb 182
Rachel Ehrenfeld 183
William Casey 184
Bill Gertz 184
Tony Blankley 185
Musa al-Qarni 187
Emilio Mola Vidal 190
Vidkun Quisling 190
Jean Raspail 191

SUBJECT INDEX

Eschatology, definition of 02
Koran 03
Hadith 03
Minor signs 04
Major signs 04
Biblical eschatology, an overview 04
Bible and Koran, different arrangement 12
Eschatology, summary of Islamic 12
Sunni 13
Shi'a 13
Signs of the coming of the Mahdi 15
Mahdi, definition of 16
Sunni view of the Mahdi 17
Shi'a view of the Mahdi 17
Mahdi, descendant of Mohammed 18
Mahdi, features and character of 18
Mahdi, military leader 19
Mahdi, authenticity of 19
Mahdi, a covenant maker 20
Mahdi, rider of the white horse 20
Mahdi's army with black flags 21
Mahdi, conqueror of Israel 21
Mahdi, miraculous provider 22
Mahdi, the archaeologist 23
Mahdi, traditions about 23,24
Antichrist, definition of 26
Antichrist, man of sin 28
Antichrist, son of perdition 28

PERSONAL INDEX **219**

Antichrist, biblical references to 28
Antichrist, man of peace 29
Antichrist, covenant maker and breaker 30
Antichrist, exterminator of Jew and believers 31
Antichrist, changes times and laws 32
Antichrist, hater of Israel 33
Antichrist, capturer of Jerusalem 35
Antichrist, demise of 36
Battle, last 37
Satan, defeat of 39
Similarities between the Mahdi and the Antichrst ....
    Deny the trinity 40
    Deny the father and the son 42
    Deny the deity of Christ 43
    Deny the cross 44
    Both are deceivers 45
    Both claim to the Messiah 46
    Both work false miracles 47
    Both ride a white horse 47
    Both change the times and laws 48
    Both deny women's rights 49
    Both rule over ten entities 50
    Both are the source of death and war 51
    Both a god of war 53, 54
    Both honor their god with gold and silver 56
    Both condone rape 62
    Both usher in a seven year peace treaty 63
    Both deceive and destroy by peace 65
    Both desire world domination 66
    Both lead a Turkish-Iranian invason 6
    Both practice beheading 69
    Both desire Israel's destruction 74
    Both occupy the Temple Mount 79
    Both enjoy desecrating dead bodies 80

Dead bodies, desecration of in Islam 81
Antichrist's final solution 76
Adolph Hitler and Islam 77
Holocaust, Ottoman Empire 78
Muslim denial of beheading 71
Decapitation in Islamic theology 72
Anti-Semitism in Islam 78
Jihad, understanding the meaning 58
Crusades 59
Antichrist, nationality of 60
Jesus, references to in the Koran 86-88
Hadith, references to Jesus 89-91
False Prophet and Muslim Jesus, comparison of 91
Jesus, references to in the Bible 93-96
Dajjal, identification of 98
Dajjal, description of 98
Dajjal and the last war 100
Muslim's view of the last war 100
Second Coming of Jesus, Hadith's teaching of 101
Signs of the end, Islamic teaching 103
Signs of the end, biblical teaching 104
Antichrist's Empire, nations of 107
Gog and Magog 08-110
Gog and Magog, location of 110
Meshech and Tubal, location of 111
Northern Confederation 110-112
Armageddon, battle of 112
Islamic Empire, its beginning 117
Revived Roman Empire, arguments against 118
Revived Islamic Empire, proponents of 120-122
Europe, demise of 123
Revived Islamic Empire, arguments for 124-126
Day of the Lord, definition of 127
Muslim nations, Christ war with 128-131

PERSONAL INDEX   **221**

Day of the Lord, according to Joel the Prophet 132-135
Judgment of the nations 136
Israel, benefactors of are blessed 137-138
Israel, enemies are cursed 136
Mystery Babylon ....
    definition of 139
    location of 139
    characteristics of 141
    religious influence of 142
    wickedness of 143
    wine of 143
    wealth of 144
    slaughterer of the saints 144
    destruction of 145
    warning for foreigners to flee 146
    identification of 147
Beast, of Revelation 149
    Identification of 149
    Description of 149
    Killer of the Two Witnesses 149
    Demise of 150
Revived Islamic Empire, the Caliphate 154
    Aspiration for a revived Caliphate 154
    Pro-Caliphate groups advance of 155
    Threat to the West 156
    Result in all out jihad against the West 156
    Turkey, headquarters of 157
    The eighth Empire 157
Turkey Mediator between East and West 159
    Key player in negotiations with Israel 160
    Move toward Islamism 160
    Military might of 161
    Anti-Semitism of 161
    Anti-Christian of 161

Takeover by Islamists 162
Place in Islamic prophecy 164
Islam not Rome is fourth beast 164
Great Apostasy ....
    Prophecy concerning 168
    Time of 170
Church in the last days ....
    Description of 170
    Decline of 170
Stockholm Syndrome 170
Persecution ....
    Prophecy of 172
    Islamic command to kill 173
    Expectation of 173
    Cause of 174
    Case of 175
    Endurance of 176
Struggle between Islam and Christianity 178, 179
Rise and fall of Islam 179
Resurgence of Islam 180
Saudi Arabia's incursion into America 180
Principles of terrorists 181
Wahabbism 181
Muslim Brotherhood Movement 182
    Father of 181
    Spiritual leader of 182
    Popularizer of 182
    Goals of 182
Terrorists in America ....
    Bases of 183
    Treasury aids terrorists 183
    Lax security measures 184
    Hindrances to fighting terrorists 185

Al-Queida ....
       Birth of 184
       Growth of 184
Islamists' plan to destroy America 187
Timetable of Osama Bin Laden 189
Fifth Columnists among us 190
Quislings among us 190
What can stop Islam 191
What can our government do to stop Islam 193

ORDERING INFORMATION

Islam and the End Times
Can be ordered from

Truth Publishers
P.O. Box 1408
Taylors, SC 29687

Or wegurganus@gmail.com

1 copy	$15 postage paid
2 copies	$25 postage paid
5 copies	$50 postage paid

Other books by Gene Gruganus

Peril of Islam – Telling the Truth

Path to Truth and Freedom – Guide for Seekers of Truth

1 copy	$10 postage paid
2 copies	$15 postage paid
3 copies	$20 postage paid
5 copies	$25 postage paid

All three books for $25.00 postage paid
Make checks payable to Truth Publishers
Pay online with Paypal   - wegurganus@gmail.com

CPSIA information can be obtained at www.ICGtesting.com
227167LV00002B/1/P

9 781935 507208